DR. SAMSON GICHUKI

Elevate Your Perspective

Raise Your Vantage Point to Get More Out of Life

Copyright © 2022 by Dr. Samson Gichuki

All rights reserved. No part of this publication may be reproduced, stored or transmitted in any form or by any means, electronic, mechanical, photocopying, recording, scanning, or otherwise without written permission from the publisher. It is illegal to copy this book, post it to a website, or distribute it by any other means without permission.

Dr. Samson Gichuki asserts the moral right to be identified as the author of this work.

Scripture taken from the New King James Version®. Copyright © 1982 by Thomas Nelson. Used by permission. All rights reserved.

First edition

This book was professionally edited, formatted, and typeset by Roy Kamau.

This book is a masterpiece any leader or aspiring leader should add to their library. In it, Dr. Samson Gichuki provides the blueprint and road map to elevate your perspective, develop a growth mindset and cultivate traits essential to your success. If you apply the insight and wisdom shared in this book, you will surely reap the tremendous benefits of a life of impact. This is a page-turner and a book that will challenge your thinking on so many levels.

Dumbi Mabiala
Author, Speaker, Founder of Mentoring Generations LLC

Short, simple, but yet powerful. Too many people are distracted by the noise in their environment and fail to live on purpose. Dr. Sam has marvelously interwoven nuggets throughout the book to serve as a guiding compass to help its readers navigate from where they are to where they really want to be. I can truly say that Dr. Sam's book contains the value of 10 books combined, and anyone that will dare to apply the simple truths in the book will be transformed.

Dipo Adesina
Author, Licensed Financial Professional, Consultant

Elevate Your Perspective touches on the brass tacks that add up to a fulfilled life. It clears all the haziness one may have to try to work out how to progress in life. It effortlessly intones: Perspective and Attitude are teeth on the cogs of destiny. Your perspective is your reality - master your perspective, master your life!

Richard Mbuthia
Author, Poet, and Teacher

Having known Dr. Sam Gichuki for several years through The Maxwell Leadership Team, I can attest that he's an exemplary leader who leads by example. He lives out what he practices, which is evident to anyone who has interacted with him. Elevate Your Perspective is a must-read for anyone desiring to grow and turn their dreams into reality. It is a timely, practical book on self-leadership and Personal Development. Do you have a desire to make an impact? Read this book.

Essie Daniel
Leadership Trainer, and Executive Program Leader
Maxwell Leadership Team

I dedicate this book to all the teachers who have shaped my perspective over the years.
To Mrs. Maina, as a teacher, you helped me have a new perspective on my potential.
To my wife, Betty, since you came into my life, you have always helped me improve my perspective, and I'm deeply grateful for you.

Contents

Foreword	iii
1 Perspective: Defines Your Reality	1
Truths about Perspective	2
The Power of Perspective	7
Pillars of Elevating Perspective	11
Unlocking Possibilities	12
2 Progress: Desire To Move Forward	17
Truth About Progress	18
Big Ideas into Big Results	21
Breaking New Ground	26
Build Endurance	30
Finish Line	35
3 Growth: Develop Yourself	39
Personal Growth Blueprint	41
Create Growth Experiences	44
Tools for Personal Growth	49
Relationships for Personal Growth	54
4 Attitude: Internal Yet Powerful	59
Attitudes For Success	63
Maintaining A Great Attitude	68
The Cost of Poor Attitude	70
Diseases of Attitude	73
5 Relationships: Don't Go Alone	78
Courage in Relationships	79

Courage To Serve	83
Courage to Lead	87
6 Productivity: Effort to Impact	93
Energy Maximizing Habits	98
Time Maximizing Habits	102
Make a Difference with Action	107
7 Faith: See Into The Unseen	112
Traveling Light	116
Power of Forgiveness	121
Unlocking More Blessings	125
The Path of Gratitude	126
About the Author	131
Also by Dr. Samson Gichuki	132

Foreword

I feel like I've known Samson all my life. As a friend he has been there for me in word and in deed. He has taught me that true friendship is transformational, not transactional. He always finds a way to make an impact with one simple approach, *"How can I add value here?"* This question has not only catapulted him to become a person of immense value, but also has shaped and elevated my perspective in ways I cannot imagine.

His desire to see people grow and be their best is a trait that few have. He is always ready to take on new challenges believing that the breakthrough he makes will help others. Because of him I have learned that perspective is a key feature in anyone's life and develops as we grow through life.

As a writer, he brings all these traits to the table as he writes about a subject that I have seen him live out over the many years I have known him. This book doesn't smell like a library, but like a chef's kitchen whose flavor has simmered over years of experience.

He will use stories from his own life to highlight the value of perspective and why it is something worth giving your attention to daily. Samson will also walk you through the path of elevating your perspective by opening your eyes to the reality of where you are and lovingly challenge you to see what you could be with a new perspective.

Like small course corrections over time can lead to a different perspective, small changes made consistently over time can lead to a higher quality perspective. Similar to an expert builder laying a foundation and bricks to create a strong building, Samson makes a case why perspective is foundational to life and proceeds to lay six powerful bricks that will elevate your perspective and give you a vantage point that looks past fear, anxiety, hopelessness, and other barriers that blur our view.

When COVID-19 hit and the lockdown happened, our church had to find a way to hold services virtually. There were many obstacles to overcome to set up the virtual system, but I saw the value of an elevated perspective as I observed Samson navigate the myriad of challenges that came with standing up this system practically overnight. I also witnessed the importance of relationships as he found the solutions necessary to ensure our church services continued without interruption. His elevated perspective kept him pressing on to discover the possibilities despite the obstacles.

If anyone is qualified to write a book on perspective, it is Samson. I have seen him exemplify what he writes over and over again. Reading this book will be the best investment of your time and the results are proven because Samson is a living example.

Are you ready to elevate your perspective?

—Pastor David Waiyaki

1

Perspective: Defines Your Reality

> *"Your perspective will either become your prison or your passport."—Steven Furtick*

If a pilot sets an aircraft to fly for a six-hour flight from Los Angeles California to JFK International Airport in New York and doesn't adjust the flight controls for the duration of the flight, the aircraft will most likely land in Miami Florida, over 1,500 miles south of its intended destination. Despite advances in aircraft avionics systems, pilots are still needed to continually monitor their aircraft movement and perform course adjustments in order to arrive at their correct destination. Failure to do so will lead to an aircraft heading to the wrong destination or worse yet, crashing in the middle of nowhere. Course adjustments correct the drift caused by external forces such as wind and gravitational pull, ensuring the aircraft remains on the right course.

Like an aircraft, you can agree that there are many forces that can make you drift away from your intended goals and purposes in life. Similar to how a pilot performs course corrections, you must take the pilot seat in our life and routinely make course adjustments in order to achieve your goals and live out your purpose.

The one thing that has helped me and I believe will help you to remain on the right path and focused on what's important, is to maintain the right perspective.

> ***Without a good view of where you are and where you're going, it is impossible to make any course adjustments.***

Perspective is the ability to assess the true nature of something, develop a mental model, and draw a conclusion that acts as a reference point. Have you ever looked at a painting, or a piece of architecture and thought, *"Wow! Whoever painted it was amazing?"* The reason why art becomes great is that it brings out the meaning of something; whether it is visual, auditory, or performing. To have a good perspective in life, you need to become a better artist. The only difference is that you will be drawing conclusions and developing mental modes, shaping your experiences in life.

Truths about Perspective

We all have experience. As we go about our daily lives, we are constantly drawing images on the canvas of our minds. Nevertheless, we can all improve on the quality of our drawings; we can enhance how we look at life and transform our experiences. You might ask, if being good at having a great outlook on life was so obvious, then why do most people struggle to have the right perspective and in turn ruin their lives? The answer can be found in three simple truths that are often overlooked.

In any area of your life, without grasping these truths, you will never be able to improve. These simple yet profound truths are:

1. Your perspective is a product of your attitude.

Have you ever attended concerts or sports games in a stadium or auditorium where you had to choose your seat? My guess is that you were keen on choosing the position with the best view of the arena. Consciously or unconsciously you understood one thing, where you sat determined your vantage and overall, your experience of the performance.

Being in a big auditorium watching a performance on the stage is synonymous to how you live life. Just as where you sit in the auditorium determines how well you view what's happening on stage, your attitude will determine how well you perceive life, your relationships, your experiences, your work, and even your purpose. Attitude is simply the mental posture of the mind. So, with a poor attitude, you can never have a good perspective.

I once heard a story about a boy named Jeb who grew up in Alabama. His mother would come in every morning at 5:00 AM to wake him up.

And when she would wake him up, she'd say, *"Jeb! This is going to be a great day."*

Jeb was to wake up to help his mom with the chores in the morning. The house was cold and he was supposed to get the fire going. But Jeb was getting tired of his mom coming in every morning saying, it's going to be a great day.

Finally, she came in one morning, woke him up, and as routine, she said, *"Oh, Jeb, this is going to be a great day!"*

He looked at her and said, *"Mum, this is going to be a terrible day! I am tired, it's cold, I don't want to get up."*

Her mum looked at her and replied, *"Sweetheart, if you feel like that, why don't you go back to sleep."*

Jeb looked at her in disbelief and wondered, *"why have I not thought of this before?"*

About three hours later, Jeb woke up to a house that was warm and filled with a good breakfast smell.

He went to the kitchen and said to the mum, *"The house is warm, the breakfast smells so good, I am hungry."*

The mother looked at him and said, *"Sweetheart, you don't get any breakfast this morning."*

"What do you mean?" Jeb was puzzled.

She continues, *"remember when I woke you up this morning I said it is going to be a great day and you said, no mum going to be a terrible day? As your mother, I will do my best to make it a terrible day."*

She sent Jeb back to his room and had to stay there all day. He could not go out or play. By the time night came, he had slept all he could. Learning from this lesson, the following morning, at 5:00 AM, Jeb was wide awake and dressed, when his mum walked in, Jeb threw his arms up and said, *"Mum, this is going to be a great day!"*

Through this story, you can see that your attitude is a choice and it not only shapes your perspective, but also your experiences.

What can you do to make sure your attitude is at its best? Similar to how you choose the best seat in an auditorium, find the best position for yourself mentally each morning. First, consider carefully the information you are consuming. If you are feeding your mind with negativity, then your attitude will be negative, and you will always have poor perspective. Second, find experiences that foster boldness to see more than you're accustomed to. I make it a point to attend events with like-minded people who encourage me to see beyond my present conditions and challenge me to pursue my wildest dreams. I believe that despite what we have experienced in the past, we can improve our attitude and in turn improve our perspective as we face life. Keep in mind that your attitude defines your perspective and your perspective shapes your experiences.

2. Your perspective shapes your reality.

Is it possible to have a lot of money in the bank and still be unhappy? Can a person be in a room full of people and still feel lonely? The answer is yes. Most of the time we miss to see the true magnitude of things because of a blurry perspective. Other times we have an accurate perspective which leads us to better understand things and we end up successful.

It's not what others think of you that limits you, rather it's how you think and see yourself that does. If you see yourself as small and inferior, you will always find excuses not to try what you perceive to be above you. But when you see yourself as capable and gifted, then you will always do things that are beyond your means. It's also true that what you look for is what you find. So, if your view or perspective is positive, your environment will be filled with positivity. When your perspective is always negative then all that surrounds you will be negative.

Wayne Dyer once said, *"If you change the way you look at things, the things you look at change."* He understood that perspective shapes our reality. Therefore, always keep in mind that your world is a rest of your perspective.

> ***It's not what others think of you that limits you, rather it's how you think and see yourself that does.***

3. Your perspective determines your impact.

The difference between how an excellent person does things and an average person is based on how they view things. When you ask an excellent person to do something, their mental posture enables them to see things in two ways; the good way and the better. The average person knows that things can be done to their best ability and not to the highest quality. This difference in attitude explains why those who have high impact, the excellent people, and those with low impact, average and below, have very distinct perspectives.

While an average person views things from a lower perspective, an excellent person has an elevated perspective. This is the basis of the statement, how you view things determines how you do things. A classic example of how perspective makes a difference is in the epic battle of David and Goliath.

While others saw the giant Goliath and became immobilized, David saw the God he served and what he had in his hands; a slingshot and five smooth stones that he could use to make a difference.

Perspective will determine your impact in two major ways. First, it will determine if you find solutions and possibilities where others only see problems and hindrances. Second, it will determine if you are a leader or a follower. People with good perspectives take on leadership. They also see opportunities before others, and go further than everyone else. Poor perspective only reduces your visibility and makes you focus only on yourself. Therefore, to be among those who have the greatest impact, those who find solutions in every problem and lead others to victory, choosing a good perspective is the way to do it.

> *Choosing a good perspective is the way to increase your capacity to find solutions and increase your impact.*

The Power of Perspective

The story of an Italian-American World War II POW featured in a 2014 film, Unbroken, portrayed the resilience of the human spirit shaped by perspective. Louis Zamperini was from a poor family and he was a troubled teenager. He didn't speak English, which made him a target of bullies in school. His older brother Pete, had him join his high school athletics' team to prevent him from being a rebel. In 1936 Louie qualified for the Summer Olympics in Berlin. Towards the final few laps of the 5000-meters contest, Louie was straggling behind other runners when he remembered, "A moment of pain is worth a lifetime of glory" a statement told by his brother during training. This instantaneously transformed his perspective of the race, which drove him to push himself in the final lap, running it in a spectacular 56 seconds, an Olympic record that stood for decades.

After the Olympics, Louis enlisted in the US Army Air Corps during the Second World War in 1941. He was deployed to the Pacific frontier, assigned on a B-24 bomber. During a search and rescue mission, their airplane experienced mechanical difficulties and crashed into the Pacific Ocean killing all but three crew members. Louis was among the survivors. After 47 days of drifting in the open ocean, Zamperini and a fellow survivor were captured by the Japanese Navy and transferred to POW prison camps where they were starved, tormented, and tortured. To survive prison cruelty, a shift in perspective marked by the words, *"If you can take it, you can make it,"* uplifted his spirit and birthed in him great resilience that kept him unbroken until the war was over.

Whether I am watching the trees slowly swing on a breezy day through the windows of my office, or standing by a beach on a vacation observing the waves crashing on the shores, I am always amazed by the force of the wind. When I see the leaves get piled up on a windy day in the Fall or the devastation brought by a twister, I marvel at the power of the unseen wind. I wonder, if the wind that is unseen can cause such a significant effect on the external environment, what unseen forces affect who I am?

I believe that wind is a constant reminder of the power of the unseen forces that act in our lives. So far, we have been looking at perspective, one of the major unseen forces that shapes our lives. Like the wind, your perspective is powerful enough to shape your life.

Let's examine three major areas where the unseen force of perspective is exerted.

1. Your Posture

After the crash, Louis and two of his surviving crewmates, Russell Phillips and Francis McNamara found themselves trying to survive on an inflatable boat. Of the three men, Francis was the only one who died at sea. What was interesting about him was that he was the only one who confessed that they were going to die. Also, the six chocolate bars they were to share, Francis selfishly ate them all while the others were asleep. On the other hand, Louis was the one stopping him from believing they would die. What was apparent was that Francis' outlook made him hopeless and desperate, and quenched his spirit long before he physically died.

Our perspective determines our posture in life. Like sitting upright or wearing the right shoes promotes good physical posture, **good perspective facilitates good mental posture**. Likewise, poor perspective hinders a healthy posture. In life, if your perspective is not right, then you will live for now. You will always seek your own interests and in the end, have only lived a limited life.

Therefore, choose your perspective wisely, just as Louis did while lost at sea and during prison.

2. Your Relationships

Your relationships define your level of effectiveness and success more than your grittiness or giftedness. Choosing your relationships correctly and investing in them is essential to success. Perspective dictates your relationships with others. Whether it's your close family and friends, or your professional relationships, perspective will shape them all. *It is your perspective of people that determines the quality of your relationship with them.*

How exactly does perspective outline your relationships? Your perspective of a person will decide whether you place their value at ten or at one, ten being the highest value, and one being the lowest. Those with an elevated perspective place a ten on others while those with a lowered perspective place a lower value. Simply put, the first way perspective affects your relationships is how you value others. Remember that *the value you see in people determines the value you receive from them, which affects the depth of those relationships.*

Your perspective will make you a person who is either easily offended by people or always grateful for them. In a group of people who have a common purpose, such as a team at work or members of a church, it's easier to identify a person who doesn't get along with others or one who has great relationships. Often, the people who don't get along with others get easily offended because they magnify people's shortcomings. While those with great relationships are grateful for the people around them because they magnify the good deeds of others. In summary, the second way perspective affects your relationships is in what you choose to focus on in others, whether good or bad. *It's not what people do to you that gets you, it's how you view them that does.*

> ***The value you see in people is the value you receive from them and that affects the depth of the relationships.***

3. Your Fulfillment

At the center of a fulfilled life is the right perspective of where one is (presently), how far they have come (their past), and how far they can go (their future). The right view of where you are currently makes you appreciate what's working and think of how to improve what's not working. This helps you to live in the moment without complaining. A right perspective of the past makes you appreciate your efforts, strengths, support systems, and struggles. Understanding that it wasn't easy, but you've made progress, enables you to live a life of gratitude and not grief. Finally, the right perspective of the future makes you look at your potential and opportunities, creating an anticipation for success within you. While a good view of the future ignites faith, a poor view ignites fear. Perspective shapes your feelings of fulfillment. *Remember that your perspective determines your appreciation, which in turn, determines your fulfillment.*

> ***Your perspective determines your appreciation, which in turn, determines your fulfillment.***

Pillars of Elevating Perspective

Is there a specific person, teacher, friend, or parent who had a transformational impact on your life? Who helped you unlock your potential?

It took me about two decades to fully appreciate the impact of my second-grade teacher on me. Her words of encouragement, and welcoming personality made me feel valued. Her reassuring smile made me know that my second-grade exams weren't the end of the world. It's because of her that I wear eyeglasses.

My glasses are a constant reminder of a teacher who believed in me at a very tender age. Thanks to her genuine interest in me, at a time when there were no preschool-eye check-ups, she realized that I had vision challenges and recommended me for an eye checkup. Correcting my vision transformed my life. Shortly after, my performance improved, and my self-esteem and confidence soared. Although the prescription glasses corrected my physical vision, her words of encouragement and caring personality acted as my corrective lenses of my mental sight. Knowing that you need corrective lenses is the first step to elevate your perspective.

Unlocking Possibilities

"The power to question is the basis of all human progress."—Indira Gandhi

It is interesting that the older we grow, the less we ask questions. We accept the systems and paradigms of the way things have always been done. We don't question the status quo, even though we are sick and tired of it. We accept our lives instead of creating our lives. I have learned that questioning is a surprisingly powerful tool for breaking new ground in our personal lives and in the society at large. We unlock value when we ask questions.

After my vision was corrected, I realized that I was as gifted as other kids and my grades weren't the true reflection of my potential. I started believing in a greater destiny. This led me to start asking focused questions on how to grow into what my new perspective brought into view. *If fixing your sight is the first step to elevated perspective, then asking the right questions is the precise tool you use to unlock new possibilities in our lives.* In the book, *The One Thing,* Gary Keller and Jay Papasan summed up the power of questions by stating, *"How we phrase the questions we ask ourselves determines the answers that eventually become our lives."*

Let's look at three ways that you can correct your lenses to elevate your perspective.

1. Know Thyself.

"The unexamined life is not worth living."—Socrates

Often, people go through life without ever realizing what is possible. They go through life with poor self-image and low self-esteem because they fail to see the value in themselves. The quote above from Socrates hints at how to live a worthy life. It begins with looking in the mirror; self-awareness.

Self-awareness is the key to knowing ourselves. A person who isn't conscious of their potential, capacity, and giftedness will always have a poor perspective of themselves and their environment. *Being self-aware means knowing what God created you with and what He created you for.*

> **A person who isn't conscious of their potential, capacity, and giftedness will always have a poor perspective of themselves and their environment.**

Knowing yourself is vital to elevating your perspective because by being self-aware, you can distinguish who you are from what you are going through or your current state. Knowing yourself elevates your perspective because to know yourself will require you to raise your view of who you are, above your current conditions. The moment you look at yourself beyond your present performance and challenges, you'll start to realize that you can do better because you were created for more. When this happens, your self-worth will appreciate in value. Soon, you'll experience a drastic shift in how you view things. Your environment will improve and the people around you will have greater meaning. In short, to elevate your perspective is to know yourself, which begins with self-awareness.

2. Seek Wisdom.

A young king took over his father's kingdom at a time when the kingdom was facing both internal and external conflicts. Without much experience, he knew that he needed more to rule a divided kingdom with many foes. Fortunately, God appeared to him in a dream and told him that whatever he asked for, he would be given. Weighing his inexperience as a leader and the task of ruling his people, he knew he needed something to help him see better. Without hesitation, he asked for wisdom. In the end, he was the wisest and wealthiest king who ever lived. His success attracted rulers from other regions to learn from his great wisdom.

Like the young king, we can agree that sometimes life brings challenges that we lack enough experience to face. Other times, we face decisions that require more wisdom. Somehow, we know that if we were wiser on how we lived we would be better off and could have done some things better. Wisdom is the gateway to an elevated perspective. It enables us to see beyond the surface and clears the smog that clouds our decision-making process. We get wisdom when we seek it. I believe the true source of pure wisdom is God. When we seek it from Him, He gives us wisdom that cannot be found in books. His wisdom enables us to have a higher standard of living and increase our odds of being successful.

> ***Wisdom enables us to have a higher standard of living and increase our odds of being successful.***

3. Invite Others.

I was once very bitter with a friend of mine. I had found out that they had said some things about me that weren't true. The bitterness was pushing me to confront him in the most unfriendly way possible. Can you relate? Before I confronted him, I met with one of my mentors and shared my predicament. In the meeting, through wisdom, she systematically enabled me to look at the issue with a new perspective. The new perspective was higher than what I had prior to speaking with her. The elevated perspective caused the bitterness to evaporate and I chose to forgive and let go of what my friend had done. That day, I learned that when we invite the right people into our world, they improve our outlook.

Nothing will elevate your perspective like surrounding yourself with eagles: people with elevated perspective. The old adage, *"Two heads are better than one,"* is a reminder of what happens when we come together. When we share our viewpoint with positive people, we improve our outlook. They fit us with corrective lenses and equip us with great questions that allow us to see things from an eagle's view. Build what I call a think-tank: A group of friends who are your go-to-place for brainstorming. Have mentors and coaches who will help you when the stakes are high. And remember inviting others is like having compound eyes that broaden your field of view.

When we invite the right people into our world, they improve our outlook.

2

Progress: Desire To Move Forward

"You don't make progress by standing on the sidelines, whimpering and complaining. You make progress by implementing ideas."—Shirley Chisholm

If you love basketball, seeing LeBron James or Stephen Carry on the court increases your heart rate slightly. If you are a soccer fanatic, Lionel Messi or Cristiano Ronaldo might keep you up late at night watching them play. If you love books, authors like Stephen King or Toni Morrison mesmerize you with their writings. And if you desire to be a mover and shaker, then leaders like Entrepreneur and Inventor Elon Musk, or activist Tarana Burke, would be your icons.

The names of the people above and other great men and women who have risen to the top in their field have been the source of many great books or documentaries on how to be successful. We are fixated on their stories. Their stories resonate with something deep within us. They inspire us and make us believe we too could be successful. But as much as we love their stories, and are gravitated to hear their successes, we tend to ignore the process they went through to be who they end up being. The reality we ignore is in their progress. We want their happiness without their process.

Living a happy life is not as difficult as we make it to be. Yes, that's right! It's not difficult. What makes happiness so elusive is how we think about it. We oftentimes think that happiness is something we qualify for at our destination. The truth is happiness doesn't need to wait until we finish the journey. I have learned that we can increase our state of happiness in life if we tie happiness to progress. In fact, I believe this is the natural way it's supposed to be. Tony Robbins says, *"Progress equals happiness."* I believe it because there is no destiny without progress. Progress is what promises us a destination.

This is why I want us to explore four stages of progress. These steps are:

1. Big ideas to Big Results: Conquering an elephant
2. Break New Ground: Mastering Rocket Science
3. Build Endurance: Sticking with the process
4. Finish Line: Ending well

Truth About Progress

Before we jump in and examine the four states, I would like us to first look at two fundamental truths about progress. Missing these truths prevents many people from ever experiencing the joy or fruit of progress. Grasping and applying them in any area of your life, will make it easier for you to overcome the barrier to progress in any endeavor, be it in your business or personal life. So, here are the two truths:

1. It's not easy but it's worth it.

"Anything worthwhile is uphill."—John Maxwell

My mentor, John Maxwell, always reminded us at the John Maxwell Team, a team of coaches and teachers that John personally trains. The nature of progress that makes it unattractive to many is that it's not easy or as my former school teacher would put it, *"it's not a cup of tea."* Progress calls for you to change your state; to move from our comfort zone and familiar territory to the stress zone and the unknown. It makes us move from what we are used to, to something unfamiliar.

I remember the early few months after I went back to get my doctorate degree being the most challenging. This was due to the fact I had to leave my full-time job to focus on my coursework. I left the safety of biweekly paychecks to the unfamiliar territory of applying for academic grands. It was also challenging because I had to read more new scientific literature to find a good dissertation project. However, the process made me discover an important truth: Any venture that leads to growth and achievement will always call for anyone to stick with progress. But what helps to keep on is to remember that progress is worth it.

What is exciting about making progress, even when it is not pleasant at the moment, is remembering that in the end it's worthwhile. Think of it like planting a tree that only produces fruits after months of hard work cultivating. Speaking of fruits, as many don't appear overnight, you might not see the outcome of progress overnight. Therefore, not expecting it to be easy and seeing it's worth it, will make you be intentional about progress.

> *Any venture that leads to growth and achievement will always call for anyone to stick with progress.*

2. It's not automatic.

While progress is impossible without change, it does not work like change. If you don't do anything about directing your life to living your purpose or use your gifts, change will still take place; Time will pass, and you will get older, but you won't get better or achieve any results. Making progress is not automatic.

A big mistake often made by people is thinking that the passage of time guarantees improvement. Too often people sit around and think that because they are getting older, they are getting better. That's not true. It's by coupling time and process that we see progress. By developing a process, you start to see how a complex task could be achieved in simple steps. with a process mapped out, it is easier to start.

Time + Process = Progress.

Mark Twain is quoted saying, *"The secret of progress is getting started."* Getting started means you have to know where you are going and what you need to begin. Intentionality is what's required to start what's not automatic. You become intentional when you take time to consider the journey that you must begin to see the results you want. It's by accepting that progress is not easy but worthwhile with intentionality that you actually achieve success in life and be happy along the way. These two truths about progress are important to keep in mind so that a few months down the line you won't be seated in the same place you're today.

Big Ideas into Big Results

About 20 years ago, space exploration wasn't a mainstream undertaking. Sending shuttles to space was reserved for governments and military operations. The few private companies that were involved in space exploration were not known because they didn't cause any significant ripples to be noticed. All this changed when a young South African entrepreneur came into the picture.

In 2002, at only 31 years old, Elon Musk founded SpaceX, an aerospace manufacturer and space transport services company. What's amazing about Musk's space venture was his approach. By the time he founded SpaceX, NASA, the leading space government agency, was struggling with funding. Public opinion about space exploration had shifted and the budget for NASA had been reduced. Their approach to building rockets was not helping them either.

In order to tackle the gigantic mission for which SpaceX was intended for, Elon Musk employed a thinking he had learned from his Physics background. He referred to it as **First Principle Thinking (F-P-T)**. This approach of thinking led him to ask himself, *what are the fundamental requirements for space exploration?* He realized that using old space shuttle parts could save him money. He also knew that manufacturing his own rocket parts would be much more cost effective than outsourcing. Eighteen year later, SpaceX is the leading private space exploration company in the world.

What's true and applicable to us is understanding that the first step to doing great exploits (doing something that has never been done before and breaking new grounds with our lives), like Elon Musk, is shifting our mindset. I am convinced that everyone, including you, has at least one big idea, with great potential that isn't exploited. And you can sense that if you worked on that idea, it would transform your life, people around you would benefit, and the tide of history would change for the better.

The challenge is when you look at the idea, whatever the idea is, like starting a business or pursuing your life's purpose, you see the work it will take. At times it can feel like you are battling an elephant. You are unsure how to turn that big idea into the results you envision. I have observed that for ideas to be turned into big results, what I refer to as conquering an elephant, one must apply the F-P-T approach to progress from idea, what is unseen, to results, what is visible. This approach involves three steps, which are:

1. Equipping.

The first step to applying the F-P-T approach to conquering your elephant idea is asking yourself *what tools are required for turning big ideas to big results?* This question allows you to discover what tools or resources you need to make progress. Often, people with valuable ideas don't make an impact because they are often not well equipped. Your best ideas will remain in your head if you haven't equipped yourself with the suitable skill set, tools, or people to help you turn them into reality.

Being equipped means having what is required to turn your

specific idea into reality. Being equipped might mean acquiring a special skill or building a team of like-minded people. It might mean having a certain amount of capital or aligning yourself with collaborators. A common trait among people who make a significant impact and make a difference in life is that they know how to equip themselves.

Whenever you have an idea that you want to actualize, your first question should be, *"What do I need to have to be successful?"* Once you have come up with a list of items you need, go search for them. You may need to buy equipment or hire an expert in that specific area to be in your team.

I have also realized that equipping begins with the carrier of the idea. In business it begins with the vision carrier. And it begins with personal growth. The rate of turning ideas into results is directly proportional to your personal growth. People who are determined to develop themselves daily and hone their skills will have more of their ideas turned into results. If your growth is limited, your progress is limited as well. But if you are equipped but lack a plan to execute, you won't see any results.

> ***The rate of turning ideas into results is directly proportional to your personal growth.***

2. Planning and Executing.

The second step to applying the F-P-T approach is by asking yourself, *what plans do I need to have in place and how am I going to execute them?* Big ideas often take extended time to materialize. They also require consistent action to turn them into something visible and tangible. Planning is taking into consideration the time of the process and the actions required at specific stages of the process to see progress.

Brian Tracy, author of *The Gift of Self-confidence*, stated that, *"a clear vision, backed by definite plans, gives you a tremendous feeling of confidence and personal power."* Planning allows you to see the actionable steps to turning your ideas into results; it increases your confidence to execute.

The best planning approach that I have found to be effective takes three things into consideration. First, determine the minimum and maximum amount of time a task or a goal will require. The maximum time acts as an upper limit and the minimum time as a lower limit. This clear demarcation of time enables me to work at a productive pace. Second, determine who will help you in doing what. Identifying potential support in advance allows you to ask for help early and reduces the chance of being turned down. Third, determine potential setbacks. The journey of turning your ideas into results, has potential setbacks. Considering them in your planning helps adjust quickly and keep moving without much delay. Remember, failing to plan is planning to fail.

3. Calibrating.

The final approach where you can apply F-P-T is in taking in to consider the changing of times and circumstances. Here the F-P-T approach leads you to ask yourself, *are my plans up-to-date, are my tools still effective?* Calibration is the adjustments done to your plans and actions to ensure you are progressing effectively in the right direction. It's impossible to increase your effectiveness without having the ability and willingness to adjust. Times and circumstances change, tools get outdated, and sometimes a new team is required to go to the next level of success. Calibrating often is necessary in the process of turning your big ideas to big results.

The best way to calibrate your progress is by asking relevant and current questions. I use these three questions to calibrate my progress:

1. Are the skills that I have matching the problems that I am facing?
2. Are the people in my team well equipped to face the current challenges?
3. Am I on the right trajectory towards my goals?

I have found that calibrating often makes progress easier and smoother.

You might not be as rich as Elon Musk, you might not be planning on space exploration, or you might be feeling that you are too old to turn your younger self ideas into big results. I want to assure you that regardless of who you are or what stage you are in life, if you apply the *First Principles Thinking* approach in the three areas we have covered, you will be on the way to turning your big ideas into big results. If Colonel Sanders, founder of the Kentucky Fried Chicken, turned the idea of a *"secret recipe"* for frying chicken into a multi-billion dollar franchise at the age of 65, I believe you have great potential for success.

> ***Calibration is the adjustments done to your plans and actions to ensure you are progressing effectively in the right direction.***

I urge you to get a sheet of paper or a journal and write down the ideas that you believe need to be turned into big results. Next to the ideas apply the thinking approach we have learned to answer these questions; what skills do I need? and who can help me turn my idea into results? I am sure this practice will lead you into a journey that in the end you will be glad you took.

Breaking New Ground

Once in college, I ran into a friend while walking to the university library. We had just finished taking the second exam in Physiology class.

"Where are you headed to?" I asked.

"To change my major," she replied.

This was a conversation that most students can relate to. My friend was struggling in her Physiology Class. She didn't have any hope of passing the class, so she wanted to change her major.

Interestingly, on further inquiry, I learned that she always wanted to be a medical doctor, but now a single class was standing between her and her dream. I told her if she wanted, I would help her study for the third exam and if she didn't pass then she should go ahead and change her major.

About two years after the conversation, my friend called me and asked me to join her for lunch. Few minutes into our lunch, she could not hold the news she wanted to share. She told me that she was currently in medical school pursuing her medical degree. She reminded me of the time I stopped her from changing her major to settle for a degree that wasn't in alignment with her dream. She was grateful.

Since I learned of her success, I became intentional about encouraging people to keep making progress even in the face of challenges. Whenever I meet people struggling with pursuing their dreams due to failure in one area or another, I always remember my friend's story and encourage them to stick with their dream. I help them to have hope like I did with my friend. This is because challenges are not meant to make you change your course but to make your resolve stronger. They are meant to strengthen you for the next challenge.

I have discovered that the greatest barrier to progress is the inability to handle challenges or solve complex problems. Whether you are a college student, or a professional who works for a company to solve real life problems, or an entrepreneur, if you can't learn complex things, or if you can't solve difficult challenges, your progress will be blocked. Often people settle for less in life because when they are faced with complex problems they quit. But your ability to learn hard tasks is fundamental to not quitting and breaking new ground. That is why I want to share with you three simple yet effective things that I have found to be useful whether in my Ph.D. pursuit or handling personal challenges.

1. Believe: Believe you can do it.

The reason why we often give up when faced with challenges is due to lack of faith. Believing you can do something activates your creativity and gets you engaged. It doesn't matter what you are facing, be it a mathematical problem or a financial problem, believing enables you to have the right mental posture. Not believing closes your mind up. It prevents you from moving forward and makes you feel stuck; a condition I refer to as mental clenching. I have observed that the people who have faith in possibilities, approach every problem believing that there is a solution and that they have what it takes to find it.

Believing in possibilities is something that we have to practice. You can increase your believing power by always staying positive, being open to new ways of approaching life, and surrounding yourself with people who have greater faith than you. If you surround yourself with people who are negative, who see a problem in every situation, and only see life from one vantage point, then your mind and heart will become weak. At the appearance of a problem, whether big or small, you will opt on giving up before even giving any effort.

The moment you start believing you can handle a challenge, that's the moment you begin to see options and new ways of moving forward. This gives you the courage to face the challenge and depend on your great friends to solve any problem, any time.

2. Time: Allocate maximum possible time.

Time is the second most powerful resource, after your brain, to solve any problems. All the rocket science challenges you will face will require time. Living in a microwave society has really affected our expectations. We expect even the things that require time to come to us fast. I have observed that we can use technology to find solutions faster than we used to but to be a master at anything will require time. You can google all your assignments, or you can watch a YouTube video on how to fix your financial challenges but to do well in the exam you will need to put in the time for practice. You will need time to build in financial discipline to be financially successful. In any challenge you face, you must allocate the maximum time needed.

The way to do this is by following two guiding steps. One, determine the best time to handle the challenge and schedule it. This helps you not to procrastinate. Second, manage the time you allocate for facing complex things. This helps not to spend unnecessary extended time on one task. Time allocation to facing a challenge allows me to be systematic and tactical in the face of a challenge. This approach has also helped me know when to ask for help; when to collaborate with others.

3. Collaborate: Rely on a team.

The third approach to solving your rocket science problems is by relying on others. Ray Kroc, the founder of one of America's most successful business empires, McDonald's, is quoted saying, *"None of us is as good as all of us."* Kroc knew to make business successful, he had to learn from and depend on others.

Another entrepreneur giant who understood the power of collaboration was the late Steve Jobs. Despite his brilliance, he knew that he needed the best people to make Apple Inc. as successful as it has been. He said, *"Great things in business are never done by one person."* This is true for business as well as our personal lives. Having a team in college to study for exams is as effective as having a team that you brainstorm with on the challenges of life. Over the years I have developed and invested in a few key relationships that help me to navigate life. Whenever I have an important decision to make, I depend on them. At work, I have a team of professionals who we work alongside each other to come up with smarter ideas and solve problems.

Together with learning really hard and complex stuff, collaboration is a powerful means through which to gain wisdom from people who are better than you. John Maxwell, leadership expert, says *"If you want to go fast, go alone. If you want to go far, go together."* Collaboration is what accelerates results and makes rocket science learnable.

Build Endurance

You're not limited!

Over and over in the history of mankind, there have arisen men and women who have reminded us of our potential as the human species. On a misty Saturday morning, October 12, 2019, in Vienna, a Kenyan marathoner, Eliud Kipchoge, broke the two hours marathon limit. Before Kipchoge took on the challenge of running a marathon in under two hours, it was almost unimaginable that any human being had the capability of running for twenty-six miles at an average pace of 4.3 minutes per mile. Experts who often studied others but never put themselves in a challenge thought it was humanly impossible to run at that speed for two hours. But years ago, another unimaginable athletic feat had been accomplished.

On May 6th, 1954, Roger Bannister, a British middle-distance athlete did what doctors believed would collapse the human heart due to pressure. He ran a mile in four minutes. Interestingly, Bannister ended up being a neurologist, studying the organ that epitomizes the human potential; the brain. He is quoted as saying, *"It is the brain, not the heart or lungs, that is the critical organ."* These two men of different races and backgrounds are a great reminder of our potential and will always stand in history to remind us that we are limitless. Studying their lives only reveals what's at the heart of progress.

While working with Men Impact Change, a non-profit organization that identifies and honors men in the community who are positively shifting the culture and bridging the gap of economic disparities, I noticed sticking quality of all the men who have been honored in the last years; they had all endured hardships and beaten all odds to be successful and impactful. Like Eliud Kipchoge and Roger Bannister, as a person of impact, you will discover that endurance is at the heart of all human progress.

Endurance is the ability to stick through the pain of progress with the sight of glory at the end of the process. Endurance is what will make you show up the next day after having a bad day today.

William Barclay, a renowned Scottish Author, once said, *"Endurance is not just the ability to bear a hard thing, but to turn it into glory."* I am convinced that if we are going to reap the rewards of what we put our minds to do, the fruits of progress in life, we must learn how to build endurance. We must take on life as a marathon.

> ***Endurance is the ability to stick through the pain of progress with the sight of glory at the end of the process.***

There are three essential ingredients that are at the core of building a life of endurance. Let's examine them below.

1. Discipline.

The best metaphoric description of discipline was provided by the late Jim Rohn, American entrepreneur and author, when he said, *"Discipline is the bridge between goals and accomplishment."* It is impossible to make progress, to move from goals and aspirations to results and accomplishments without having a disciplined life. Discipline is developed by knowing three things.

First, you ought to know what you want. This helps you have a reference point. When Eliud Kipchoge decided that he would one day break the two-hour barrier, he elevated his training regimen despite having one of the best training practices given that he is the most decorated marathoner in history. When you know what you want, you shift how you approach life.

Second, you ought to know what it takes to achieve what you want. Often most people spend too much time talking about what they want instead of finding ways of how to achieve what they want. Identifying what it takes for progress to be made is a result of preparation. And preparation is what reinforces your will power to remain disciplined.

Third, you ought to know the impact of what you want when you achieve it. This is visualizing the glory of what you want once you achieve it. A good example is provided again by Eliud Kipchoge. In his quest for running a sub-2-hour marathon, it was clear that he knew the glory was not him being recognized but making it known that no human is limited.

What's one thing you want to achieve in your lifetime that will require you to live a disciplined life? Answering this question will help you live a focused and unclenched life.

2. Focused and Unclenched.

The second critical piece that is at the substratum of endurance is focusing and unclenching.

Towards the end of last summer, one Saturday morning, my friend David and I went for a run. As we were running, I was struggling to keep up with him - admitting I was overweight - when he moved closer to me and said, *"Remain unclenched and focus on the upcoming hill."* Those words were like a rocket booster to me. I felt a fresh burst of energy from within and I made it up the hill. That day I ran longer than I had done in the whole summer and made a counter intuitive discovery; when you focus on what's important, it helps you remain relaxed and calm (unclenched). This helps channel our energy in the right direction and on the most beneficial task at hand. This alignment of energy and what's important allows endurance to be developed with ease.

Focusing is possible when you have the right perspective. In a world of constant distraction, knowing what's important and true is the best way to shape your perspective and maintain focus. Also, surrounding yourself with like-minded people will help you remain focused on what's important and true. Once you find your focus, it's easier to unclench and allow all your effort to be directed at what will produce the greatest results. Tony Robbins' quote, *"your life is controlled by what you focus on"* always reminds me of the importance of focus.

What's one area in your life that you need to focus on? And what's one area of your life you need to stop focusing on? Answering this question is not only important to finding your focus and remaining unclenched but also fulfilling your purpose.

3. Purpose.

The third essential ingredient to building endurance and supports the first two ingredients is purpose. Purpose is what helps you connect what you are doing to the larger world. It's what makes what you are doing have meaning and impact more people. Connecting your goals and aspirations in life to something bigger and greater than yourself is the sure way to elevate your sight above the current challenges and difficulties. It helps you see more and do more. It gives you hope and zeal to always get better.

One of the best three-point shooters in the NBA, Steph Curry, has linked his performance on the basketball court with saving lives in Africa. He collaborates with a foundation that donates a mosquito net that prevents malaria in Africa. For every 3-pointer Curry made, three insecticide-treated bed nets are donated. This act made Curry's shots reach far and beyond the basketball court because it is connected to purpose.

My journey to being a better person has made me connect what I love doing, speaking and writing, to a life of daily finding ways to add value to people around me, including you through this book. I have seen my endurance grow in all areas of my life. This has led me to another discovery. Endurance is a muscle that when developed in one area of your life, can transform all other areas of your life. So, the final question for you is, what purpose do you need to connect to what you love doing or your calling in life?

We can agree that endurance is important if we want to see progress in our lives, especially on the important things that move us closer to our destiny. I strongly encourage you to take time on the three questions I have asked you at the end of each section. The depth of your answers to the questions will determine the depth of your endurance. Lastly, I will leave you with this advice by Roger Bannister, *"The man who can drive himself further once the effort gets painful is the man who will win."*

> ***Endurance is a muscle that when developed in one area of your life, can transform all other areas of your life.***

Finish Line

I love nature. The spectacular landscapes created by the American Appalachian Mountains, the Great Plains of Africa, and the Great Barrier Reef, the world's largest coral reef system. They are all amazing and fascinating, but what I find most powerful and remarkable are the great rivers of the world, like the Nile, the world's longest river. It is so powerful that it transforms every land it passes through.

A river is symbolic of a transformative process that begins small, but as it progresses its impact is massive. The greatest impact of a river is felt at its end. It forms a geographical feature known as a delta; a finger-like feature formed as a massive river branch out to form distributaries that drain the water into an ocean or lake. At a delta, all the sediments, the fertile soil, that were collected as the river flowed downstream are deposited. This is why the delta region is most fertile for farming and home to varied wildlife.

In any process or journey of life, like a river that ends at a delta, you can reach the end and harness the value you have accumulated along the way. The experiences, lessons learned, and wisdom gained could be the fertile ground to plant your next goals in life and avoid the pitfalls of many one-hit wonders. This is when you can say you have crossed the finish line well.

As you have learned in the last sections, there are different stages of progress that you must go through to see the fruits of our hard work. You must have the ability to turn big ideas into big results, learn complex and hard things, and have endurance in life.

Now, I want to share with you how to end well; crossing the finish line, the final stage of progress. I believe that the end of progress is important because it determines if you are able to have serial success. That is, as you close one process and start another, you are able to keep producing more success.

There are two things that facilitate serial success: a growth mindset and an attitude of gratitude. It is important to retain these as you cross the finish line in any race of life.

1. Growth Mindset.

For a long time, I was planning my life around my goals. All this changed after turning twenty-nine. I was working at my first corporate job in a field that I went to college for. One afternoon, as I was taking a *"reflection walk,"* it hit me that I had accomplished all my major academic and professional goals; I was exactly where I had planned to be in life. But then, I quickly noticed danger lurking ahead.

I observed that most of the people I was working with at the company were quite successful; the majority had advanced degrees and were working in good positions. However, they also seemed to be unsatisfied. Their dissatisfaction was evident by their daily complaints about their careers. The danger was being trapped in a career that I had worked hard to have. This was as a result of living by goal-mindset versus living by growth mindset. Don't get me wrong, goals are fundamentally important, but they have to be based on a long-term growth plan.

A growth mindset is essential and most importantly, when facing a transition, because of three main reasons.

First, a growth mindset allows you to look back and analyze your experiences. This turns your experiences into a school. You look at your successes and ask yourself what are the key decisions that made your success possible. You also look at your failures and ask yourself what you would have done differently to avoid the failure in future.

Second, a growth mindset allows you to look at your present stage and analyze your present opportunities. Often, one-hit-wonders, people who succeed once, miss to look for opportunities when they hit their success. They party longer and when they are done celebrating, they feel the weight of going back for the next race to be a great burden. They settle for succeeding once and that's all they are known for. Anytime you are successful at anything, don't stay on the podium too long, but rather go back and train for more battles and successes.

Third, a growth mindset allows you to look forward with anticipation. You look forward to applying whatever lessons and wisdom you learned in your past to your present and future opportunities.

I can assure you that a growth mindset will assure that you achieve all your goals and live a purpose driven life. When you start living from a growth mindset, not only will your approach to progress get transformed, you will experience a shift in your attitude. You will begin to have an attitude of gratitude in every step of your journey, especially when you approach the finish line.

2. Attitude of Gratitude

The most challenging part of any progress is finishing well. Most people quit right before their breakthrough. It is when you approach the finish line that you need to put all your effort. Often, discouragement looms in the last half of the race. What I have discovered is that when you are on the final stretch of any process, it is the attitude of gratitude that enables you to mass-up the last ounce of energy to make it to the finish line. An attitude of gratitude reminds you of three things.

First, it reminds you of the people who have come along the way to help you get where you are. You remember who is on your team and the people who are cheering you on. Lack of gratitude often can make you feel like you are all by yourself and makes you susceptible to discouragement before crossing the finish line.

Second, it helps you realize the great opportunity you have had to be in the race despite the pain you have gone through or are still going through. As I am working on my PhD. I realize that an attitude of gratitude is important to remind me of the opportunity I have had to be a PhD. student. This has helped me to remain on course.

Third, an attitude of gratitude allows you to be a giver. Once you are grateful it is impossible to be selfish. Gratitude makes you want to share with others the valuable lessons you have learned along the way and to provide support to others who are on the same journey you are on. This helps you to cross the finish line with others. Those in front of you become your mentors in the next race and those behind you become your mentees.

Finally, an attitude of gratitude will help you discover that success and satisfaction intersect at the realization that it is God who blesses you with the ability to do what you do. And it is the people around you, who support you in what God has enabled you to do. I myself, am grateful to God and to you.

3

Growth: Develop Yourself

"Personal development is the belief that you are worth the effort, time, and energy needed to develop yourself."—Denis Waitley

Personal growth is a topic that has been extensively covered, but millions of people around the world have not yet realized its impact. The process of intentionally growing or developing yourself has the profound effect of unlocking our potential to become the best version of who we were created to be. Growth is the foundation of all human achievement and success.

   Whether you want to excel in a personal goal such as becoming the best artist, leader, entrepreneur; or if you want to do something that positively impacts the society at large; or if you want to make your organization operate more efficiently, personal growth is the bedrock for turning desires into results. Personal growth assures us that our futures will be better than our present and past. When we devote ourselves to a lifestyle of growth and personal development, we have the means to live the life we eagerly dream.

It's not the lack of purpose that frustrates us, it's the inability to fulfill our mission that does. It's not the inability to set a goal and act on it that makes us feel powerless; it is when we look at our unfulfilled goals that drains our passion. Personal growth provides the means to fulfill our purpose and accomplish the goals we set. And the incentives of personal growth are beyond achieving one goal, personal growth ensures our capacity to fulfill our purpose and attain success in life is always filled. Your life's purpose and the things that you would like to do that will bring you great satisfaction, demand you increase your capacity by committing to a life of growth.

If I were to be asked when I became intentional about personal growth, I would say it was May 27th, 2015, the day I earned a master's degree. However, when I look back, I realize that personal growth did not start in 2015, it began much earlier. It began when I decided to never be the last in my class in middle school. I started on a personal growth journey when I challenged myself to go for the highest level of formal education. At the time, I did not have a name for it, I just wanted to get better.

Looking back, it was in those formative years that unlocked my purpose and began living purposefully. I don't come from a family of people who were privileged to pursue higher education. As a matter of fact, when writing this, I have no knowledge of anyone in my family who stepped into college. However, because I was purposeful, I went from getting Ds in middle school to earning a Phd.

Upon completion of my Master's degree from the Honors University in Maryland, I quickly observed that many adults were unhappy regardless of their education or their careers. I realized that many people had accepted their lives and given up on their purest childhood dreams. They had retired their creative souls and settled for what the society defined for them; their careers, their zip codes, and their class. Why did this happen? Because many people got trapped in a fixed mindset trap, that made them believe that their circumstances are set and the only thing they can do is to be comfortable where they are. You must avoid this trap at all costs.

Personal Growth Blueprint

Our greatest hindrance to a life of personal growth and development is the lack of life's blueprint, or having one that's not well thought out. The legendary civil rights leader, Martin Luther King Jr., shared three pillars which he believed were essential to a life's blueprint while speaking to the graduating students in Philadelphia. Even though Dr. King didn't mention personal growth in his speech, I believe that these pillars are important to a blueprint that will lead to a lifetime of growth.

1. A deep belief in your own dignity, worth, and somebodiness.
   The first pillar to our life's blueprint, according to Dr. King, was a deep belief in one's dignity, worth, and uniqueness. This pillar hit on three crucial elements that are at the root of personal growth and development: self-worth, purpose, and significance. The third law of growth, The Law of the Mirror, from John Maxwell's book, The 15 Invaluable Laws of Growth, states, *"You must see value in yourself to add value to yourself."*
   Dr. King emphasized the necessity of us having a deep belief in our own dignity or self-worth. He understood that we couldn't grow if we don't see our true worth. When we see our

value, we discover our purpose. I have observed that people who have found their purpose in life actively seek ways to develop themselves. They understand that their purpose is always higher than where they are. Therefore, they need to grow to fulfill their purpose. A clear observation of anyone's purpose, including yours and mine, uncovers another truth. A purpose-driven life always achieves to live a life of significance. Once we fully or deeply believe in our own dignity, worth, and somebodiness (a word coined by Dr. King), we activate the second pillar in our life's blueprint, a determination to achieve excellence in all our endeavors.

2. Determination to achieve excellence in your endeavors.

A question I have recently been asking myself is this: What is one thing that I can do or can be doing that I could be considered world-class in? As I explored this question, I discovered one important truth. Whatever anyone can do to be considered world-class, there must be an element of excellence in his or her work. But excellence doesn't come naturally. We have to strive to be excellent. I believe this is why Dr. King said it must be a determination to achieve excellence in all endeavors.

When we have a determination to achieve excellence woven into our being, three things will happen. *First,* we will always be optimistic and determined to improve anything we do. *Second,* we will have a never give up spirit. We will always see anything through to the end, no matter the degree of difficulty. *Third,* we will always stand out. In a world where competition is fierce and full of mediocre work, the only way, which has always been the best way to move above the pile is to be excellent in any work you get to do.

There is only one secret to achieve excellence, which is tucked in a Bible verse that says, *"Whatever your hand finds to do, do it with all your might"* (Ecclesiastes 9:10, NIV). All your might means all effort or strength, which includes your mind, soul, and body. To do this, you have to possess an attitude that Scripture says, *"Whatever you do, work at it with all your heart, as working for God, not for human masters"* (Colossians 3:23). Why God? Because when your work is connected to a power greater than you or something supernatural, that's when your work will make a difference.

Dr. King promised that when we have the determination to achieve excellence in our endeavors, then not only will the world respond, but even heaven and the heavenly host will notice. But the determination to achieve excellence is not going to be possible without the third pillar in our life's blueprint, a commitment to the internal principle of beauty, love, and justice.

3. Commitment to the internal principle of beauty, love, and justice.

It is impossible to grow consistently and fully benefit from your growth plan if your mind is jammed with negative thinking. This third pillar that Dr. King pointed to is instrumental in orienting our minds to positive and power thinking.

People such as Dr. King, Mahatma Gandhi, and Nelson Mandela who fought inequality and sacrificed much for their fellow countrymen to be awarded a fair playground for their economic and social prosperity, not only had a commitment to the eternal principle of beauty, love, and justice, they also committed to growth. They understood that only when we have an eternal perspective of beauty, love, and justice, can we have hope. And where there is hope, there is positive thinking as well.

What are these eternal principles? The eternal principle of beauty is understanding that you're beautiful, and everyone else is as beautiful as you are. And love, know that God loved us first, and we are to love one another. And justice is knowing that everyone is to be treated with fairness. This third pillar allows us to live beyond ourselves. It enables us to grow and desire growth for others.

It's important to examine what's in your life's blueprint carefully. In essence, you need to see whether the foundational principles you live by are allowing you to grow or preventing you from growing. The litmus test for growth is how you handle life's challenges and the quality of your relationships.

While having a blueprint is important to building our best lives as we desire and deserve, we need to have a goal to build. Think about an architect who draws a beautiful building that would serve an important purpose, but right after finishing his drawings, he locks them away. Would the building ever get built? Will it ever fulfill its purpose? This is also the case with us. If we don't have goals that produce growth, our blueprints will be worthless.

You have to set goals that produce growth experiences.

Create Growth Experiences

How many miles can you run per day, or how many books can you read in a month? Or how How many miles can you run per day, or how many books can you read in a month? Or how much money can you earn per year? The answers to these questions are dependent on how much you're willing to stretch yourself. Your growth determines your level of performance and achievement.

A few years ago, I made a goal to read one book (besides what I read for work) per month. I selected the twelve books which I would read for the year. But four months down, I found myself getting frustrated because I was falling behind my goal. Another time I made a goal to run a hundred miles per month and the same frustration of not hitting my goal set in when I realized I couldn't make a hundred miles. Determined to achieve my hundred miles per month goal, I decided to give myself another month. What was different in the second attempt was that I did more miles than the first attempt. This was when I discovered something important that has made me, in the past, not successful in my goals. I realized a gap existed between where I was and the success I wanted to achieve in my goals.

This gap is called the growth gap. Lack of awareness of the growth gap leads to frustration and throwing in the towel when we experience the pains of achievement. Filling this gap begins with one desire.

I recently read *The One Thing* by Gary W. Keller and Jay Papasan. In this classic book, Keller and Papasan present a simple truth, simplifying workload by focusing on the one most important task in any given project is the secret behind all extraordinary results. This book has equipped me with the tool for boiling down everything I need to do to one thing, which, if I handle well, everything else will fall into place. I have applied this principle to achieve growth in all areas. When it comes to all my goals, I have discovered that the one thing I need to focus on is growth. And to bridge the growth gap, the singular desire that I must have is the desire to grow. The desire to grow in every experience you go through in life is the key to making all your experiences beneficial. So, to turn your goals into growth experiences you must focus on these four areas:

1. Growth mindset.

In her book, *Mindset,* Dr. Carol Dweck, Ph.D. describes two types of mindsets, growth-mindset, and fixed-mindset. Dr. Dweck describes a fixed mindset as a self-perception or "self-theory" that people hold about themselves, which makes them believe that their basic qualities, like intelligence or talent, are fixed traits, and can't be improved upon. Also, fixed-mindset people believe that talent alone creates success—without effort. On the other hand, she described the growth mindset as self-perception that makes people think that their basic abilities can be developed through dedication and hard work; intellect and talent are just the starting point. Growth-mindset people have a deep desire for learning and a resilience that is essential for great accomplishment. Growth-mindset is the first important thing you must possess when you're developing and setting your goals.

When you possess a growth-mindset at the front end of your goal setting, three major things will happen. *First,* you will set goals that will stretch you. Your current capabilities won't limit you because you understand that you can always improve your skills and talents. *Second,* you will not be afraid to be challenged. Dr. Dweck's research shows that people with a growth-mindset view challenges as exciting rather than threatening. So, when you have a growth mindset, you don't think that challenges will expose your weaknesses, but reveal your strengths. *Third,* you will always have the right questions to ask for maximum growth. For example, Dr. Dweck says that questions such as, "*Did I win? Or did I lose?,*" after an experience are the wrong questions. Instead, the best question should be, "*Did I make my best effort?*" The difference between the right questions and wrong questions is the level of commitment to improve they ignite in you.

Growth-mindset is critical since it enables you to focus on effort and progress, which will be essential to stay focused on reaching your desired outcomes.

2. Outcomes.

One of the hallmarks of highly effective people, as outlined in Stephen R. Covey's book, *The 7 Habits of Highly Effective People,* is that they begin with the end in mind. In all endeavors, productive and successful people begin their journey with a clear understanding of their destination. They know the outcome they want to see. The second item to keep in mind for your goal to turn into a growth experience is defining your desired outcome.

To clearly determine the outcome you want, it means you have to know where you want to go, understand where you are now, and the reason why you want to change. When you have outcomes determined, three things will happen.

First, determining the outcome you want to see helps you count the cost and manage your resources well. Cost doesn't necessarily mean money, but it could mean a system that you have to put in place or the relationships you must develop. When you predetermine your outcome, you focus your resources for maximum impact.

Second, it will help you decide a course of direction and remain focused on it. Covey calls it, *"making sure your ladder is leaning on the right wall."* Without clearly defining your desired outcome, you might become busy on things that won't get you anywhere close to achieving your goals. *Third,* with an outlined outcome, you will know when you arrive at your key milestones. This makes it easier to celebrate and feel fulfillment along the journey to achieve your goals.

The overall benefit of clearly determining your outcome (beginning with the end in mind) is that you can set your attitude, which is the third critical element for turning goals into growth.

3. Attitude.

While attitude cannot compensate for skills, it drastically improves how you do everything. Attitude is the mental posture that leans either on the positive or on the negative. When it leans on the positive, it becomes your greatest asset in achieving your goals. When it leans on the negative, it becomes your most expensive liability in anything you do.

Our attitude determines two essential things when it comes to turning goals into growth experiences. *First,* it allows us to understand that life is 10% what happens to us and 90% how we react to it. With a positive attitude, we accept this truth. With a negative attitude, we reject it; we begin to blame instead of taking responsibility for our outcomes. *Second,* our attitude determines our learning capability. The ability to learn from your experiences is the fuel to your progress. With a positive attitude, you will be able to stay longer and work harder on your goals. You will do what I refer to as going the whole-length.

4. Length.

How far are you willing to go to see your dreams become

a reality? This is the commitment question. After deciding on a goal, asking yourself this question enables you to count the cost you are willing to pay on the journey to achieve your goal. To succeed, your willingness to stretch, to keep trying until it works, and dig deep into your resources, will need to be considered.

It's not the absence of passion or hard work that keeps many people from succeeding, but rather the lack of commitment. Often, when we set goals, we are blinded to the amount of time it's going to take. So, when it takes longer than what we had anticipated, we throw in the towel. To avoid this pitfall, I always answer the *how long* question with *as long as it takes*. The reason I give such a bold answer is that I am confident that with a growth-mindset, a clearly outlined outcome, a positive attitude, and a full-length commitment, I will experience success.

Therefore, the only way to increase your probability of achieving your goals is by turning all your goals to growth experiences. It's going to take a lot of sacrifices since sacrifice begets success. And there is no success without achievement. Success is the end-result, while achievement is skill, effort, and courage.

We have a blueprint and goals to build a life of growth that is a foundation to elevating our perspective. We now need tools.

Tools for Personal Growth

The only guarantee that you will be ready for future opportunities is by preparing for them today. Your level of readiness will determine your level of success in any endeavor. I have observed far too many people wishing for success, but not realizing that unpreparedness is their greatest liability.

Personal growth, the process of intentionally improving yourself, is the surest way to be ready for tomorrow's opportunities and challenges. You will only be better tomorrow by growing today. The golden opportunities you are seeking are all contained within you. They are not in the external environment. The iPhone and Apple Mac were inside Steve Jobs before Apple became a name brand. Before Microsoft became the excellent computer interphase, we all use, it existed in Bill Gates. And before Amazon became the leading online store, enjoying the largest market share, it existed in Jeff Bezos. Personal growth is the process that allows you to bring forth the greatness that God hid in you; it is digging out the treasure within, and in the process unveiling a better you everyday.. Therefore, the greatest return on investment of your commitment to personal growth is a better future.

If anything, that 2020 historians will remember about 2020, it will be a year when systems were examined, questioned, and changed. In the wake of the death of George Floyd, the whole world was taken by a storm of civil unrest in demand for a change of systems. People from all corners of the world seem to have a collective acknowledgment that the many years of suffering caused by injustices could only be stopped by a change in systems that run our societies.

For decades, systems that have facilitated racism, and the oppression of minorities cannot be allowed to continue if we want a better society. The millennials and Gen-Zs, who were the majority of the demonstrators filling the streets, seem to have comprehended one fundamental truth; for society to get better in the future, effective systems must be in place. This truth that a better future is dependent on a robust system is also applicable at a personal level.

For us as individuals, we must set in place systems that will allow us to grow. Since growth is not an automatic process, and we should be intentional about it, we must arm ourselves with tools that will make growth easier. Three tools I always use and which I believe, if you have in your toolkit, will help with your personal growth are:

1. Design Thinking

I once read this quote by Jim Rohn that changed how I approach life. *"If you don't design your own life plan, chances are you'll fall into someone else's plan. And guess what they have planned for you? Not much."* I realized that my lack of planning for my future would lead me to coast through life being a victim of other people's plans. I began to think like a designer, knowing that I have the power to shape my life and create a future; however, I desired.

Successful people have a designer's mentality; they approach life as builders, always keeping their blueprints at the forefront of their minds and consulting them often. People who live a significant life don't drift through life; they grow through life, enabled by design thinking.

This thinking style enables us to continually evaluate our day to day life (decisions, actions, and experiences) in reference to these questions; What do I want my life to look like? What do I have and need to build a life that I want? And what am I doing today that will get me to where I want to go in life? When we have this mindset, we tie our core beliefs and values to our goals and aspirations. Our life is marked by creativity, productivity, and positive change. It's when we practice design thinking that we can unlock the next tool for personal growth, comprehensive questioning.

2. Comprehensive Questioning.

I love to ask questions. If there is one thing that I am glad I didn't lose from childhood is the boldness to ask a lot of questions. The only difference is that the quality of my questions has become better as I grow older. In his book, *Good Leaders Ask Great Questions,* John Maxwell says, *"Asking questions is a great way of preventing mental laziness and moving ourselves out of ruts."* To that, we can add that questions unleash our mental strength that shows up as creativity. I have observed that people who are successful in any field have the ability or skill to ask questions with a deep desire to understand something (situation or a person) fully. I refer to this skill of asking questions as comprehensive questioning. They ask questions that lead to a deeper understanding of the situation they face.

Great questions that are comprehensive have four qualities. They are clear, concise, relevant, and purposeful. I abbreviate them in the acronym C.C.R.P. Growth questions must be clear. A clear question begets a clear answer. Breaking down complex questions into single-dimensional questions enables us to focus on a single idea or piece of the bigger equation. Second, great questions are concise. To achieve conciseness in asking questions, you must be intentional with words. Omit unnecessary words. The third thing to keep in mind is to make your questions as relevant as possible. I have found that when I ask relevant questions, I get relevant applicable results in the area I want answers. Finally, a comprehensive question must be purposeful, which gives it value. You must achieve something meaningful with each question you ask. I believe that all purposeful questions in the area of personal growth must at least seek both innate and specific knowledge and stimulate thinking.

Questions are essential to experiencing a change in life. For maximum growth, we must develop the skill of asking great questions. The quality of your question determines the quality of your solutions. Tony Robbins once stated, *"Quality questions create a quality life. Successful people ask better questions, and as a result, they get better answers."* I believe that comprehensive questions activate the next tool for personal growth, systematic learning.

3. Systematic Learning.

Albert Einstein once said, *"Life is like riding a bicycle. To keep your balance, you must keep moving."* How do you keep moving in life? By learning. You learn when you are willing to open up to new ideas and to expose yourself to new experiences. I believe that if you are optimistic about the future and expectant of a long life, you will desire to grow through life and not to drift through life. One person who was super optimistic about the future was Mahatma Gandhi, who advised, *"Live as if you were to die tomorrow. Learn as if you were to live forever."* The greatest advantage of applying yourself to learning is that you will always remain relevant in the times you live. This is supported by Henry Ford's observation, *"Anyone who stops learning is old, whether at twenty or eighty. Anyone who keeps learning stays young."* So, do you want to stay young? You must be intentional about systematic learning, which is having a system or method of learning key areas/things in life that will significantly impact your life.

I have devoted myself to learning in these three areas; self-awareness, relationships, life-experiences. What are you learning that will help you grow so that you are ready for tomorrow? Remember, never stop learning, for when we stop learning, we stop growing.

One statement about Oprah Winfrey that encourages me to keep making adjustments to be who I need to be so as to get what I want out of life is, "We can't become what we need to be by remaining what we are." I believe that through personal growth we elevate our perspective and in turn enable us to move from where we are to where we want to be; It makes us be who we desire to be.

Without touching on relationships, personal growth can not be complete. In addition to the tools for personal growth, we need people. I believe there are key relationships that can pivot our life's experiences for exponential growth.

Relationships for Personal Growth

In 2020, COVID-19 pandemic has prompted us to change how we live in unimaginable ways. Nobody would have predicted that homeschooling would be the norm and wearing face masks mandatory while shopping at the local grocery stores. But of the many changes we had to make, nothing has been more profound as social distancing, a concept that's contrary to the core element of what makes us social beings.

As much as we increase our physical and social distance from each other to prevent the spread of the virus, we should not neglect to cultivate the essential relationships that help us improve. During the recent COVID pandemic in which I had to stay home, with limited social gatherings, I had to utilize virtual meeting platforms such as Zoom or Google Hangouts to maintain the connections with people in my life. This made me realize that I could still forge and foster relationships that mattered for my personal growth and development despite the pandemic restrictions.

My core belief is that to become better, we need to move closer to key people in our lives; people who by merely being around them our lives become better. By being closer to movers-and-shakers, the eagles who fly high during the storm, such as we are facing, we benefit from the proximity principle.

Do you want to maximize the "lucky" breaks in your life? Do you want to go further in anything you do than you have ever gone? Do you desire to maximize your influence and the impact of your life? If your answers to these questions are yes, then you must be near where the acts of success are happening, which means you have to be close to people who are succeeding in whatever area you want to experience any success.

I define the proximity principle as the distance between you and the people related to you which determines the negative or positive impact they have on you. For example, if you are close to a person who has a positive outlook on life, you will soon have the same outlook. This works in areas of skills. If you want to improve your communication or writing skills, you should hang around people with these skills and you will notice an improvement. The great Michael Jordan wanted to be great and be in the class of Magic Johnson and Larry Bird, so he cultivated personal relationships with these men. When Kobe Bryant came around as a rookie in the NBA, Jordan was the G.O.A.T., and in desiring to achieve greatness, he applied the proximity principle by cultivating a personal relationship with Jordan. What is the lesson here? If you desire to be excellent and successful, move near great people who will help you grow into greatness. How do you do this? By intentionally building relationships that matter for your personal growth. Here are three simple steps you can do starting today to benefit from the proximity principle.

1. Surround yourself with like-value people.

Growing up, whenever I went to visit my grandparents, I enjoyed playing with fire, in the literal sense. I would sit beside a fireplace and periodically pull out a piece of burning coal from the grill and allow it to sit separated from the rest. I noticed that the burning coal I had pulled out would quickly go off. And whenever I put it back with the rest of the charcoal in the grill, it would continue to burn. My conclusion was that one coal needs to be amid other burning charcoals to fully release its potential.

We can draw valuable lessons from this analogy of the burning charcoal to when people of similar values come together. *First,* the people who we surround ourselves with will determine the intensity of our passion. This is important, especially in achieving growth that leads to success in any life's mission. *Second,* we can only reach our full potential in life when we are around the right people. Dr. John Maxwell advises, *"The better you are at surrounding yourself with people of high potential, the greater your chance for success."* *Third,* only when other like-value people surround you can you do great things. Such as one piece of charcoal can't cook food by itself, but requires a collective effort from many charcoals, you too can only achieve greatness when you collaborate with others. On top of my collaboration list are mentors and coaches.

2. Use mentoring and coaching.

As you find your people, that is the like-value or like-minded people; I highly encourage you to use mentoring and coaching to aid you to grow exponentially. A mentor or a life coach is a person you are in a relationship with who intentionally guides you to see the strengths in you and help you tap into your potential.

All people who achieve great success have had mentors and coaches who helped them along the way. Coach Dean Smith, called a "coaching legend" by the Basketball Hall of Fame, was one of the many coaches who came alongside the legend Michael Jordan. Another coach was the renowned Phil Jackson, who enabled Michael to win six championships with the Chicago Bulls.

To have a great mentor coach relationship, keep this in mind. You must be ready to be corrected, want to get better, and have the ability to improve. *"He (MJ) was very inconsistent,"* this was the initial assessment of Dean Smith on Michael Jordan when he started working with him. But the coach added, *"He wanted to get better, and then he had the ability to get better."*

I believe it is when we surround ourselves with people whose values resonate with ours and work with mentors and coaches that we can become people of positive impact as the great Michael Jordan.

3. **Be a person of positive impact.**

The more I study successful people; I have come to recognize a simple yet profound principle on breaking limits in our life. All truly successful people have realized that giving of themselves in doing things that will positively impact others is the way to discovering new possibilities and breaking limits in their lives. This is not only true to the super successful people who we put on a pedestal as a society, but also true in our successes which don't get camera attention.

The first way to experience personal growth is to become a

person of positive impact. If you live a selfish life, only looking out for yourself, you can only go so far before sabotaging your progress. But to expand your growth at an exponential rate, and accelerate your progress towards success, you will need to find a way to live beyond yourself by giving to others. Giving our resources only opens our eyes to the depth of what we have. Selfish living limits us from getting more resources.

To be a person of positive impact, aim to possess these attitudes daily. Begin your days believing that you can make a difference in someone's life. Look for ways that you can add value to anyone you interact with. And when you see an opportunity to positively impact someone, you immediately do it. If you possess these attitudes, you will find that you can do greater things than you thought possible. In the process, you will be cultivating relationships that matter for your growth.

In summary, in the words of Jack Canfield, the author of *Key to Living the Law of Attraction*, *"Make a conscious effort to surround yourself with positive, nourishing, and uplifting people; people who believe in you, encourage you to go after your dreams and applaud your victories."*

4

Attitude: Internal Yet Powerful

"Everything can be taken from a man but one thing: the last of human freedoms – to choose one's attitude in any given set of circumstances, to choose one's own way."—Viktor E. Frankl

Have you ever felt what is happening in your life, is only happening to you? I have. Many times, I have found myself feeling life is unfair. I saw the people around me happier than I was and wondered why I was the only one experiencing hardship. Everything I tried to do did not work as easy as for other people, I would think. The thought that the hardship and challenges I faced were only happening to me made things darker; I became despondent and lost all energy. But I remember making a simple yet transformative discovery that changed how I looked at my situations. I discovered that life happens to all of us.

Additionally, I learned, it's not what happened to me that made my life more challenging or easier, but how I processed what happened to me. I am not sure whether, like me, you have to constantly remind yourself that you are responsible for the climate in your life. I have the power to decide whether I will have summer or winter. The key thing is we all have access to the thermostats of our lives. The question is whether we know how to operate it. Your attitude is the internal factor that controls your response to your circumstances; it is your thermostat. Let's look at three important truths about your attitude.

1. Impacts my choices and shapes my circumstances.

"A fight is going on inside us," an old Cherokee said to his grandson.

"It is a terrible fight and it is between two wolves. One is evil and the other one is good," he added.

After a short pause, the grandson asked, *"Which wolf will win?"*

The wise Cherokee simply replied, *"The one you feed."*

This story is often told to teach about the raging battle between evil and good within us, but I would like to use it to point out two mental postures that are represented by the two wolves in our day to day living. Within us, there are two mentalities that fight for dominance in our lives; a victim mentality and a victor mentality. When I kept thinking that life was unfair to me, and felt disempowered to do anything about it, I quickly discovered that I was feeding the evil wolf which was evident through the victim mentality. To break this mentality, I had to choose to feed the good wolf, which according to the Cherokee was joy, peace, love, hope, serenity, humility, kindness, benevolence, empathy, generosity, truth, compassion, and faith. By continually feeding my faith, I made another crucial discovery; I was not the outcome of my circumstances, rather I was of my choices. I concluded my attitude impacted my choices and shaped circumstances; It determines our approach to life.

When our attitude is positive, we develop a victor mentality. Shifting to a victor mentality will lead you to appreciate the principle truth that most people never discover: it's not what happens to you, it's what happens in you that matters. Life is 10% what happens to you and 90% how you respond to it.

> *"The longer I live, the more I realize the impact of attitude on life. It will make or break a company, church, or a home... The remarkable thing is we have a choice every day regarding the attitude we will embrace for that day. We cannot change our past...we cannot change the fact that people will act in a certain way. We cannot change the inevitable. The only thing we can do is play on the one string we have, and that is our attitude."—Charles Swindoll, Founder of Insight for Living.*

The attitude we have is what can make a difference in our experience throughout life.

> **Life is 10% what happens to you and 90% how you respond to it.**

2. Difference Maker.

The best way to have a good day is by waking up and deciding to have a positive attitude. You can never have a good day with a bad attitude. And you can never have a bad day with a good attitude. Your attitude has power over anything that happens to you in the day.

Your attitude makes a difference in any environment you enter. It affects how you see the environment and how the environment reacts to you. Think of your attitude as your favorite perfume; if you wear it and get into a room, everyone gravitates towards you. The opposite is true, people will avoid you if you have a bad attitude. I think of a bad attitude as bad breath. Since people are a major factor in our environments, our attitudes impact our relationship. It makes the difference between having a great or poor relationship with people.

In addition to relationships, your attitude makes a difference in how you approach life in general and how you handle challenges. As we saw earlier, your attitude determines if you will have a victor or victim mindset. With a poor attitude, you will approach life with a negative outlook and see challenges as roadblocks. But when you have a positive attitude, you approach life positively; you will be full of life. Challenges will be opportunities for growth since you will be a solution finder instead of a problem identifier. But the most remarkable thing your attitude will do for you is it will make a difference in your performance. And this is where you discover the next attribute of attitude; a great separator.

3. Great Separator.

I love watching track and field during the Olympics. And I am a die-hard fan of the greatest marathoner in history, Eliud Kipchoge. But before I tell you his take on attitude, here is a question for you. What is the difference between the person who wins the first position and the one who gets the second position? If you said it's their level of skill, you are partially correct. The most complete answer that includes their skill is their attitude. I say this because when it comes to the marginal difference in performance, it's not skill that counts, it's attitude. The top best athlete and the second-best in any sports often have the same level of skills. But what separates them is their attitude. Attitude is the greatest separator in performance; it is what separates average from good and good from great. It is what will separate you from the other best candidate on a job interview or consideration for a promotion at your current job.

"Athletics is not so much about the legs. It's about the heart and mind," said Kipchoge.

In this quote, Kipchoge gives his take on attitude. He uncovers a powerful secret in a great performance. Whether in sports, at work, or in any area, the attitude of your heart and mind makes a great difference and separates you from the pack. Our attitude is a great separator because it's the cornerstone for excellence.

Before moving to the next section, here is a question to reflect on. What area of your life (make it as specific as possible) requires a change of attitude? As you identify where you need to change, remember that it's what is happening in you that matters the most.

Attitudes For Success

Moved by the need to save the diminishing bee population, five-year-old Houston Texas native, Mikaila Ulmer, began selling lemonade at her parent's house. The lemonade was prepared with her grandmother's 1940s recipe, using honey from local beekeepers. In 2015, she appeared in the television show Shark Tank, where she successfully received a $60,000 investment from Daymond John to support her idea and growing business.

At a tender age, Yash Gupta became dependent on his eyeglasses. In high school, he broke his eyeglasses and was forced to wait for a week to replace them. In that week of waiting, Yash realized the transformative impact eyeglasses had on his education. On doing some research, he learned 13 million children around the world lacked eyeglasses because they couldn't afford them. Subsequently, at only 14, he founded Sight Learning, a non-profit organization that, to date, has collected and distributed more than $1.1 million worth of used eyeglasses to students in countries such as Mexico, Honduras, Haiti, India, and the United States.

At 16, Greta Thunberg became a global ambassador for climate change. On Friday 15 March 2019, through her efforts, she mobilized 1.6 million people worldwide to hit the streets in support of the Fridays for Future climate change movement, the biggest day of global climate action we've ever seen. In the same year, she was invited to speak at the UN's annual assembly to world leaders on the danger of ignoring climate change. What can we learn from Mikaila, Yash, and Greta? The remarkable stories of these young movers-and-shakers can teach us that in spite of our backgrounds, we can do great things. You have no excuse to be a success story.

The Money Question

What would you want to achieve if money was not a problem? Before we look at successful people, and the attitude at the center of their success, we have to address what prevents most people from succeeding. Money is one primary resource that we need to achieve many things, but it should never stop us from fulfilling our dreams. The more I pursue my dreams and find ways to be impactful with my life, I am discovering a simple but profound truth about how successful people overcome the shortage of resources such as money in doing what they want to do.

Successful people in the marketplace and ministries such as churches have discovered that it's not the lack of resources such as money that stops success, but rather it is the lack of resourcefulness. When you become resourceful, the floodgates of resources open up to you. You soon realize that your attitude towards success becomes better. So, how do you define success?

> **When you become resourceful, the floodgates of resources open up to you.**

Success is something that everyone wants but is often elusive to many. While I am sure there are variations in how we define success from person to person, I believe that the fundamental elements of success are the same among all cultures and across different generations. At its most primal level, success is seeing the fruits of our effort. *"Success is really nothing more than the progressive realization of a worthy ideal."* Earl Nightingale said, and added, *"any person who knows what they are doing and where they are going is a success. Any person with a goal towards which they are working is a successful person."* With this definition as a background and also knowing that we hold the key to success by being resourceful, we can now look at the major attitude behind every successful person.

Make-a-Difference Attitude

Have you ever heard the phrase, *"behind every successful man, there is a woman"*? I grew up hearing adults say this, but I wondered who is behind every successful woman. While it is essential to have an important partner to be a success, I believe that there is an attitude that transcends gender or age, which is the driving force behind every man or woman, a Make-a-difference attitude. It is this attitude that was behind Mikaila's drive to do something about bees, and drove Yash to do something about children without eyeglasses, and definitely drove Greta to push for the world to do something about climate change. A make-a-difference attitude is what is at the center of all successful people.

I occasionally enjoy watching Shark Tank, the TV show Mikaila was able to get the investment that led her lemonade to be sold nationwide in different stores and chains. By observing all the winning contestants like Mikaila, and other successful people like Yash and Greta, I have learned that a make a difference attitude does three important things that enable success.

First, it allows whoever has this attitude to adjust their perspective when facing any challenge. Remember we saw that a good perspective is at the bedrock of a general great attitude.

Second, with a make a difference attitude, you position yourself to make a difference with whatever you have. Most people fail to achieve their goals because they focus on what they don't have and lose sight of what is in their hands. For example, most people reference the lack of money for not progressing with their goals. When you position yourself to make a difference, resources will flow your way. Third, you ignite your faith and believe in making great things happen. A make-a-difference attitude not only initiates success, it also sustains it by creating in us a servant's heart.

Attitude of Servanthood

Do you want to be great? If your answer is a resounding yes, you have to find a way to serve people. Successful people have learned that the only way to go up is by helping others. Making a difference in the world by giving yourself to global causes, such as climate change or meeting people's needs like Yash Gupta, who is continually providing eyeglasses to students in need through his organization, boils down to possessing a servant's heart. I believe that when we serve others, we find our purpose and fulfillment in life. Mahatma Gandhi said, *"The best way to find yourself is to lose yourself in the service of others."* Also, a person with a servant's heart will always have an abundant mindset. And with this mindset, you will not only expect good things to happen, but you will also be a miracle creator in your life and the lives of others.

In summary, when you have a make-a-difference attitude, there will be no limit to what you can achieve. You won't make an excuse for not having resources, but instead, you will be resourceful to others in service.

Maintaining A Great Attitude

Are you an attractive person? Think about a person you like, admire, and enjoy being around them. If you were to select one thing that attracts you the most about them, what would it be between these four choices:

a). Their appearance.
b). Their wealth.
c). Their status.
d). Their attitude.

The first three items were seem ideal until you think about attitude. We can agree people's attitudes trump their appearance, wealth, and their status. A good attitude goes a long way in deciding who we want to be associated with. A restaurant server with a positive attitude will get more tips than a server with an unattractive attitude. The best way to keep your best foot forward in unlocking potential opportunities tied to people is by always having a great attitude.

With the COVID pandemic came a lot of adjustments and working remotely was one of the significant adjustments that many people had to acclimate to across all work sectors. As a Ph.D. candidate, I was greatly impacted, to the point where I was not sure how I would successfully conduct my research, given that a huge portion of my work could not be conducted virtually. A few weeks into the shutdowns and shelter-in-place, I realized my biggest concern was really not my research, but my relationship with my research advisor (my boss). My relationship with her became strenuous, communication broke down, and tensions rose between us. I found myself always complaining about her and almost quit working with her.

> ***The best way to keep your best foot forward in unlocking potential opportunities tied to people is by always having a great attitude.***

Luckily, things changed for the better when I received a call from the Dean in June. Before the strenuous relationship, I would have graded my attitude as an A+. I have always been 'Mr. Great Attitude Guy' who is always smiling. But through the wisdom of the Dean of our school, I came to an awakening discovery. I learned that my expectation that my boss would change was causing more problems than helping the situation. I had completely forgotten it is not what happens to me that matters, but instead what happens in me.

It had been a while since I did an attitude check and adjustment. While I could have blamed the COVID pandemic stress for my predicament, I decided to audit my attitude and use the issue as a learning experience. The reflection of what had been going on led me to discover two truths about what our attitude can't do.

First, your attitude can't get better automatically. *Second,* your attitude and mind can't remain or stay great by itself. Despite having a track record for a great attitude, my past attitude did not guarantee that my attitude would be good in the future. I must put in the work to maintain a good attitude. So, we must pay the price of having and maintaining a great attitude by intentionally and diligently working on attitude adjustment as required.

The Cost of Poor Attitude

Without realizing the truths about what your attitude can't do, you might find yourself in a strenuous relationship as I was. Even worse, you might lose an opportunity to achieve your goals. The breakdown of the relationship with my research advisor would have cost me more than it would have cost her. For her, she has a Ph.D. already, and she could get another student. But for me, it would mean leaving her lab where cutting-edge research happens, delaying or forfeiting my graduate study, or either losing or having poor relationships with others who would have been involved like our Dean. The cost of poor attitude is poor performance, broken relationships, and ultimately failure to maximize our potential.

If the cost of a poor attitude is this expensive, what can you do to make sure you have and maintain a great attitude?

> *The cost of poor attitude is poor performance, broken relationships, and ultimately failure to maximize our potential.*

1. Expand and Elevate your outlook.

A change of attitude starts with a shift in perspective. I was fortunate in my situation with my boss since I got a chance to receive wise counsel from the Dean. For the past two years, I have been a graduate student at my school. I have had the opportunity to forge a good relationship with the Dean and his associates. When they heard of what was going on between my research advisor and me, the Dean took the initiative to reach out to me.

He candidly listened to my concerns and asked lots of questions. Once I finished speaking, revealing my attitude, the Dean slowly helped me develop an expanded and elevated outlook of the situation. He helped me realize that despite the sour relationship, my research advisor still wanted me to be successful. The Dean made me see other positive things my boss did for me. He also made me see my potential for success, regardless of what was happening at the moment. It took me a few days before realizing the impact of the conversation I had with the Dean. As a result, my perspective expanded and elevated, and my attitude positively shifted.

An expanded and elevated outlook helps our attitude in three major ways. *First,* it allows us to realize there is more to it than we can see. The more I interact with people, I realize that those who travel a lot, have gone to many countries or regions, and interacted with many cultures, possess a better attitude. *Second,* you get to see what is important when you expand and elevate your perspective. *Third,* people with expanded and elevated perspectives see other people's point of view, which helps them with their attitudes.

2. Surround yourself with people of great attitude.

While our attitude can deepen or break our relationships, the people we continuously interact with significantly influence our attitudes. As I have seen with what I shared with you above, my good relationship with the Dean helped my perspective and subsequently improved my attitude.

While the case with my Dean is a once in a while occurrence, the people who significantly shape my attitude are the ones I spend a good deal of time with. I have found the words of Jim

Rohn, *"You are the average of the five people you spend the most time with,"* to be true. I have been privileged to have great guys with great attitudes consistently help me with my attitude.

When dealing with the relationship issue between my research advisor and I, my mentee, a young third-year undergraduate student, immensely helped my attitude adjustment. Her outstanding attitude provided an example to emulate. Working with her, whether virtually or in the lab, greatly helped me have a great attitude. As a scientist, I would put it this way. Attitude can diffuse from one person to another, so be careful who you hang out with. Surround yourself with people of great attitude and they will challenge you to grow in the area of attitude.

> *Attitude can diffuse from one person to another, so be careful who you hang out with.*

3. Find your purpose and let it guide you.

After telling my mentor, Mr. Waiyaki, about my goals of attaining a Doctorate's degree, he has since called me *Daktari*, the Swahili name for Doctor. Over the years, I have found that he always reminds me of who I want to be and has helped me maintain a clear view of my goal and purpose. With a clear picture of what I want to achieve, I found it easier to adjust my attitude and rebuild my relationship with my boss. To have and maintain a great attitude, you must find your purpose and allow it to guide you in developing the attitude required to accomplish your goals. Purpose will keep you grounded in a great attitude. It will help you pivot faster when you drift into a poor attitude. And lastly, it will help you keep weeds away.

Having an expanded and elevated perspective will help pivot towards a good attitude. The people you surround yourself with will infuse and nurture their attitudes in you. Your purpose anchors your attitude and enables you to maintain it.

Purpose will keep you grounded in a great attitude.

Diseases of Attitude

In the recent global pandemic, the word vaccine became a mainstream terminology. People discussed vaccines around dinner tables, in churches, and on political stages. While the divide on whether vaccines are the key to handling disease still exist, I believe that there will be no vaccines to deal with an ancient human disease; the disease of attitude. There is no injection, patch, or tablet that you can take with the promise of a great attitude.

Similar to how you can be under attack from viruses such as the flu and become ill, you can suffer from an illness of attitude. Pathogenic mindsets could infect your attitude. If we consider John Maxwell's definition of attitude as an inward feeling expressed by an outward action, and merge it with the definition of mindset, which is a person's established way of thinking, we can see how a poor mindset can directly affect our attitudes.

The root of all diseases of attitude is a poor mindset. While we are wired and accustomed to being alarmed by new problems, such as a pandemic or economic recession, our wiring could be our enemy. In the recent 2020 global pandemic, the initial reaction was swift and forceful, but a few months into the crisis, people became pandemic fatigue. You can get worn down by restrictions placed to curb the spread of pandemics or systems established to revive the economy. But you can't afford to get worn down from fighting poor mindsets off your life. You must win this fight daily to keep attitude diseases at bay.

What if people paid the same attention to maintaining a healthy attitude as we do to preventing the spread of pathogens? I believe it would increase productivity and boost healthy relationships. Like any illness, the key to avoiding attitude diseases is identifying the early signs. There are many signs, but poor performance, broken relationships, and unutilized potential are the most common and pronounced ones.

All attitude diseases stem from two conditions: indifference and a distorted self-image. Let us examine these conditions further.

1. Indifference.

Jim Rohn identified indifference as the first disease of attitude. He referred to it as a *"mild approach to life."* Living a life of indifference is comparable to drifting through life, letting go of the will to do something about and with your life. Indifference is the greatest threat to living a purposeful life. It is the number one and most dangerous disease of attitude because it hinders purpose-driven life; it chokes any effort to fulfill your purpose.

Where indifference exists there is no commitment, seriousness, and no excellence can ever be achieved. Indifference expels commitment in relationships, at work, and in leadership. It even affects the commitment to personal growth, which is the prerequisite for a great attitude. When commitment is compromised, it is impossible to be serious. Indifference makes a person blind to the consequences of their actions. And when commitment and seriousness go out the window, so does excellence. An indifferent person lacks commitment to themselves, to the people around them, they don't take important matters seriously, and they never achieve outstanding work.

> ***When commitment is compromised, it is impossible to be serious.***

The most effective way to get rid of any indifference in an area of your life is to find purpose. Knowing your purpose allows you to identify what is important and act on what is critical for your success. It helps us prioritize. Purpose elevates our sense of awareness and urgency. With purpose, it's easier to keep the weeds off your mental garden where great ideas germinate. It's impossible to live a life of purpose and entertain thoughts of indifference. The danger of indifference is that it leads to the development of the second serious disease of attitude, a distorted self-image.

2. Distorted self-image.

The second deadly disease of attitude is having a distorted self-image. When you have a lower image of yourself, you suffer from low self-esteem. When you see yourself higher than you are, you become prideful. Both of these will negatively affect your attitude. So, what can we do to have an accurate self-image? Three things must be in place for you to have an accurate self-image.

First, a true identity. Who are you? Your identity will determine how you see life. A false identity means you live a false life. A true identity means you like the life you were created to live even though your external experience does not match where you ought to be. I believe our identity is shaped by what we believe our origins are. As a person of faith, I believe my origin is from God. My spirit is an extension of God's Spirit. It's in my faith in God through reading His Word (the Bible) that I define my identity. Where do you draw your identity from?

Second, a correct perspective of your past. As much as we would like to say that the past is the past, our history has a great influence on us. The influence it has could either be positive or negative depending on how we perceive. When you have a poor perspective, an outlook that's not empowering you, you will have a distorted self-image. On the other hand, when you look at your past with a good perspective, you will move towards an accurate self-image. A poor perspective of your past is looking back in your life and seeing the failures, then concluding you are a victim. With a good perspective on your past, you still see your failures but also see your strength. Your failures become learning experiences. Is your perspective working again and negatively affecting your attitude?

Third, a hope for a good future. Facing the future without hope is toxic to how we see ourselves. It diminishes confidence in our ability to create the futures we were created to live. When you feel like you can't have the future desire, your self-image becomes distorted. You see yourself as incapable and powerless. Your attitude becomes sour, but with the hope of a better tomorrow, you see yourself as strong and well capable to create the future you see through the prism of hope.

While there might be no vaccine to protect us from the diseases of attitude, we have a guard-aid (not found at CVS or Walgreens) that can keep us away from catching diseases of attitude, and also help us recover if we fall ill. Self-discipline is the antidote to indifference and the anchor that centers us on the accurate image of God who created us and is the standard of our self-image. Self-discipline comes easily when you know God has given you power over your life.

5

Relationships: Don't Go Alone

"If you want to go fast, go alone; if you want to go far go together."—African Proverb

A few years ago, I decided to be intentional in building my character. This was born out of realizing that the people with great character did not become who they were by accident. They chose their character. To start with, I picked seven virtues that would be the core of my character. These made the list; integrity, kindness, love, humility, respect, commitment, and courage.

But on closer examination, I realized that each of the above qualities depend on courage. It made the other virtues stand. Without it, I won't be able to love for love's sake, I won't respect other people's opinions, or maintain integrity when what I stand for is at odds with what is widely acceptable even though it's wrong. Maya Angelou, one of the greatest poets and civil rights activists, beautifully captured the importance of courage in regards to other virtues when she said, *"Courage is the most important of all the virtues, because without courage you can't practice any other virtue consistently."* Courage is elemental to success and wholesome living.

In her New York Times Bestseller book, *Dare To Lead*, Brené Brown defines courage as *"A set of skills, which includes rumbling with vulnerability, living into our values, braving trust, and learning to rise."* I have found Brenè's assessment of courage to be very accurate. After observing great leaders and trailblazers who have changed how we live or a teenager who I saw standing up for a friend against bullies, I realized that the four skills were in play when they portrayed what we call courage. What enables us to conquer fear is stepping into vulnerability, believing in value, trusting it will be alright, and rising above all opponents.

Being a person who values relationships, I have spent lots of time studying the importance of relationships in building a life that matters and makes a difference. I have observed that people who are truly satisfied in life, men and women who enjoy breakthrough success, all have great relationships. They are bold in making relationships that help them in their personal and business lives. So, I always ask this question: How do you bring your real self into a relationship without giving in to the fear of being vulnerable? The answer has always been developing courage.

Courage in Relationships

The strength of any relationship is dependent on three factors, the quality of conversations, the state of emotions involved, and forgiveness. Courage enables us to first, start and continue in a crucial conversation. Authors of *Crucial Conversations*, Joseph Grenny, Ron McMillan, and Al Switzer defined crucial conversations as conversations when stakes are high, there are opposing opinions, and involve strong emotions. We can agree that at one point or another we have grappled with crucial conversations. We can agree that without courage it is impossible to talk about sensitive but important matters. Fear often prevents us from opening up on things that may threaten the relationship. It can lead us to imagine the worst possible scenarios. When this happens, we feel cornered or defeated and negative behaviors erupt in sarcastic moments and violence. *Second,* courage allows us to express healthy emotions without being held back by the fears of what-ifs. Finally, courage unleashes the greatest antidote of broken and poisoned hearts, forgiveness. It takes courage to apologize, and it takes even greater courage to forgive.

The Measure of Courage

The central idea of having courage in any relationship is the welcoming of vulnerability. Vulnerability is exposing our naked hearts on the backdrop of our uniqueness. It is the matrix of our strengths and weaknesses. It is the humanness of our being. Unlike popular belief, vulnerability is not being weak but rather it's the strength indicator of our courage. It enables us to showcase who we are and bring our truest beautiful selves in any relationship.

> *"Embracing our vulnerabilities is risky but not nearly as dangerous as giving up on love and belonging and joy—the experiences that make us the most vulnerable."—Brené Brown.*

Brené Brown's quote underscores the nature of vulnerability, but to be vulnerable and build and cultivate courage in our relationships we must do two major things: unmask and embrace.

1. Unmask.

In a world of make-up, and filters, it is becoming increasingly difficult to know people's true identity. Before people post or share a picture, they take more than 20 pictures and use filters to hide what makes them beautiful, their *"imperfections."* As the world seems more connected, we are increasingly putting on masks to fit in and feel accepted.

Worse than putting on masks on social media is showing up in relationships with masks. While we might think that masks hide our weakness and spots of imperfections, they also cover our gifts and strengths which make up for a large part of who we are. As a matter of fact, masks don't cover our weakness. They manipulate them and project them in an uglier nature that shows up in pretense and a fake identity. Simply put, wearing a mask in a relationship only propagates fear.

The first step to developing courage in a relationship is taking off the mask. This might seem counterintuitive, but it's by taking the first step of overcoming fear of being seen that ignites courage in us. Unmasking means forsaking the strategy of ego and taking up humility. It's understanding that people love us for who we are and not for who we pretend to be. It's giving up trying to prove who you are not and being who you are.

It's true that when we unmask, we show our scars and wrinkles, but also, we show our stories. The scars show the battles we have overcome, and the wrinkles show the wisdom we have gained in our mistakes. It's only by removing the masks we hide behind that the people we are in relationship with embrace us completely.

While unmasking makes people see the true you and appreciate who you are, embracing yourself, draws people to you.

2. Embrace.

The next step of cultivating courage in a relationship is accepting who you are. Embracing who you are is looking into the mirror and loving who you see. It is embracing the color of your skin, the texture of your hair, and most importantly, your personality, whether you are where you want to be or not. Because,in order to become a person of value, you must love yourself and see the value in yourself. I do this by viewing myself not through the lenses prescribed by society, but through the truth of who God says I am. The question for you here is, what's your true identity? It is by seeing your true value that you're able to embrace yourself.

But you can never completely embrace yourselves without embracing others. So, as you embrace who you are, embrace others for who they are. Accept their strengths and their shortcomings. This will give you courage in your relationships.

The danger that lies in not embracing yourself fully is lack of confidence. Confidence in others and in yourself. People who haven't fully embraced themselves often struggle with insecurities. And not embracing others in a relationship will only breed unhealthy expectations and conflict.

Therefore, in order to be fully engaged in a relationship you must develop courage. This is only possible if you're vulnerable enough to unmask and embrace others and yourself. Remener, it's not what you do that brings satisfaction, but it's who you do it with and do it for that will make you fulfilled. It is the people that count and the relationships you will build in this life. So, start to unmask and embrace yourself. It will not be a one-time thing. It will be a process. Be patient and trust the process.

Courage To Serve

> *"Only a life lived in the service to others is worth living."—Albert Einstein.*

On April 1st, 1942, a young 23-year-old Desmond Doss signed up for the US Army at the heat of the Second World War. Doss' sign up and service in the Army was not an ordinary one, given that he signed up at the middle of the war. According to records, he had a deferment not to serve, which most young men were eager to do.

What's astonishing about Doss was how he served. With his dreams of being a doctor wiped away by the Great Depression, Doss joined the army as a medic. Being a devout Christian, he did not believe in taking a life. He made an oath to never touch a gun and subsequently requested the army not to issue him with one. Yes, as it might shock you now, it shocked the Army officers and fellow soldiers. How could he be a soldier and not have a gun? But his belief to make a difference by serving in a time of war made him decide, *"While everybody is taking life, I'm going to be saving it, and that's going to be my way to serve."* At the end of his service Desmond Doss had saved over seventy lives on the battlefield without shooting a single bullet. His Medal of Honor was truly a Medal of Service.

You don't have to join the armed forces to serve. You don't need to be a leader to serve. You don't need to have material possessions to serve, and you don't need to have extraordinary talents to serve. Serving is the act(s) you do that alters how others feel.

Maya Angelou once said, *"People will forget what you said, people will forget what you did, but people will never forget how you made them feel."* Two truths about service are first, everyone is serving someone. Whether you knew it or not you served someone today as long as you had any human contact. Second, at the elemental level, service impacts how people feel. What Maya implied is, your actions of service might be forgotten but the outcome of your service will never be forgotten. I believe since serving is about impacting how others feel, whether we do it consciously or unconsciously, we all are capable of serving. You too can serve.

And as Ralph W. Emerson once stated, *"The purpose of life is not to be happy. It is to be useful, to be honorable, to be compassionate, to have it make some difference that you have lived and lived well."* Serving is the channel through which we accomplish our life's purpose.

Let examine three things that you can do daily to develop courage to serve others in such a way that it will increase your impact, make a difference in the lives of others and touch people's hearts.

1. Choose an Abundance Mindset.

At a very young age, I believe that I could make a difference. I remember one time there was a very devastating drought in many parts of Kenya, where I was born and raised. The government and nonprofit organizations' efforts seemed like a drop in the ocean. News outlets were constantly reporting on how people were dying, especially in the Northern parts of the country. On a Sunday afternoon, a lady who was unfamiliar to me stood in front of the local church and announced that she and an organization she was working with were conducting a food drive. She told us where food was being collected.

On Monday morning, my dad gave me some lunch money as he was accustomed. But instead of eating lunch that day, I decided that I would go to the supermarket and buy a pound or two of flour and take it to the food drop off location, to go help those who didn't have food. What really shocked me was when I got to the food drive, I happened to be the first person to donate food. What I didn't tell you was that the lady and her team had visited many churches the previous week. But out of the people who heard the call for donations, I, a young boy at the time, was the first to donate. All you need is to have an abundance mindset.

When you have an abundance mindset, you will discover a few things. *First,* there is more than you need. Unlike a scarcity mindset, which makes you feel there is not enough for you and creates a selfish attitude in you, an abundance mindset expands what you have and enables you to see opportunities to serve and give to others. *Second*, it makes you a river and not a reservoir. Being a river means you have the ability to pour in others. You pour material things such as food and resources like money and also the most essential and most potent things that are intangible like love, hope, compassion, and empathy—the things that make us human. *Lastly,* when you possess an abundance mindset, you become a person who is full of gratitude. Gratitude and an abundance mindset feed into each other. When you are grateful you develop an abundance mindset. When you see abundance, you become grateful. Being grateful does one more thing—it enables us to be okay with the discomfort required to serve others.

2. Be okay with a little discomfort.

The one thing that keeps most people from serving others is the feeling of discomfort that comes with it. It's true that when we serve others, we will at times be inconvenienced. We will often have to go out of our own way. What I have discovered is that my service to others is greatest when I am out of my comfort zone. The more I go out of my way to help the deeper I reach into peoples' hearts. As a result, they feel loved, honored, and important. This has helped me forge some of my deepest relationships.

The moment you start being okay with a little discomfort to help someone, not allowing your position prevent you from climbing down the hierarchy, and going the extra mile, the courage to serve others will always persist. I have also learned that you can only be okay with discomfort, when you have hope for a better tomorrow.

3. Have hope for a better tomorrow.

Hope is one of the most powerful human traits that brightens the future. Hope gives us confidence to act on your beliefs. It gives courage to forget ourselves so that we can serve others. Zig Ziglar said it best, *"If there is hope in the future, there is literally power in the present."* Having hope for a better tomorrow will allow us to serve others.

When you have hope for a better tomorrow, you will see possibilities in the present and opportunities in the future. Although you may not have all that you want, God has provided for all your needs and therefore you can share. I have found God to be my true source of hope because I believe He holds the future, and meets my needs, and issues the medals of honor for serving others. What's your source of hope?

Serving others may look tiresome in the beginning or may make you uncomfortable, but along the way it turns out to be the most fulfilling endeavor you could be in. Therefore, the question to guide you as you serve others is what is the best outcome you desire for the people you're serving? This question will enable you to have an abundant mindset, sacrifice some of your comfort and have hope for a better tomorrow.

Courage to Lead

At the age of 26, he became the Prime Minister of the most powerful Empire. He is considered one of the greatest leaders who ever lived. It wasn't the success during the good times that made him stand out but rather it was when his country and the world order was threatened that made him an icon of bravery.

A mighty army led by a ruthless dictator was met with a courageous, fierce, and unwavering leader. The Nazi Germany was conquering Western Europe at a lightning speed and their victory was blazing like a bushfire. The last victory they needed to take over the entire Europe was the small Island nation of England. Sir Winston L.S Churchill took on the mammoth task of defending his nation against a power that was astronomical, against all odds of winning.

Churchill's courage was well captured in his hope infused speech that rallied his people, he said, "*We shall go on to the end. We shall fight in France, we shall fight on the seas and oceans, we shall fight with growing confidence and growing strength in the air, we shall defend our island, whatever the cost may be. We shall fight on the beaches, we shall fight on the landing grounds, we shall fight in the fields and in the streets, we shall fight in the hills; we shall never surrender.*" In the end Britain, emerged victorious and began a cascade of victories against the Nazi German. Winston became the embodiment of courageous leadership in our modern history.

John C. Maxwell, the top leadership expert, defined leadership as influence. John Quincy Adams, the sixth American President said, *"If your actions inspire others to dream more, learn more, do more and become more, you are a leader."* Contrary to popular belief, leadership is not based on positions and titles, but rather on influence. You don't become a leader when you're made a manager or a team leader, you become a leader when you influence a person. If you examine your life, you will find someone, your child, husband, or wife, or some people, your team or your employees, who are looking up to you for directions and guidance, this makes you a leader. You don't have to be a Winston Churchill, but you can develop the courage to lead the people under your influence, to encourage them to never ever give up, and like Churchill, inspire them to be bold in the face of uncertainty.

Traits of Courageous Leaders

An article by Susan Tardanico published in the Forbes Magazine outlined the traits of courageous leaders. Here were my top five:

- Seek feedback and listen
- Communicate openly and frequently
- Lead change
- Give credit to others
- Hold people (and yourself) accountable

Examining the list above, not only did I desire to possess all of the traits, I also realized that courageous leaders are in short supply. And from the principles of economics, when the supply is low the demand is high. We live in a time when there is a shortage of courageous leaders. Consequently, this has made those among us who are willing to be courageous enough to lead to be of great value. In ministry or in the marketplace, if you want to multiply your value and make a great impact in society, then you must be willing to develop yourself to be a courageous leader. Let's take a look at three underlying principles that will make you a courageous leader.

1. Personal integrity.

The number one personal goal of anyone who wants to be a great leader is to first and foremost choose to be a person of integrity. Integrity is the foundation of courageous leadership. Trust gives permission for people to listen to you and to be led by you. Integrity with people is the cornerstone on which trust is built. Integrity means being transparent to the people you lead. They see you for who you are. It is consistently behaving in a manner that is in line with our moral principles. It is admitting when we are wrong and showing willingness to change for the better as a leader. John Maxwell very well showed its importance when he said, *"Integrity is important in building relationships. And is the foundation upon which many other qualities for success are built, such as respect, dignity, and trust."* So, since this is the foundation to building courage to lead, examine and take care of your character, upon which integrity is exercised, then align your actions with your virtues and moral principles.

> ***Trust gives permission for people to listen to you and to be led by you.***

Once a leader builds trust with his people, he can now draw them closer and speak to them from the heart. Once distrust, which is the number one threat to leadership, is eradicated, people embrace the leader, and a value-based relationship is cultivated.

2. Valuing people.

It is impossible to lead people who you don't value. Every leader in history that you could think of, that's truly celebrated long after they are gone, valued people. Valuing people is loving people. It is to make everyone under your influence feel important.

Going back to Churchill, he was one of the most popular leaders during his time in office. In a scene depicted in the film, *The Darkest Hour,* directed by Joe Wright, Churchill is seen riding the London subway in a goal to find out what the ordinary Londoners thought about a heated debate of whether England would stand up against Adolf Hitler or settle for an occupation by the Nazi. Whether it happened exactly as depicted in the film is not of importance here, but history has it that Churchill valued people and what they thought, he would regularly find his way to the common people and hold what is equivalent to what we nowadays call town hall meetings. Valuing people is what gave Churchill the courage to lead his people. Even when he had to rally people into war, it was easier because he had already shown that he valued them. A leader who truly values people will cultivate a faith-based relationship with the people where the leader develops unwavering faith to lead.

Valuing people is loving people.

3. Unwavering Faith.

Unwavering faith is what makes people committed to a leader. While integrity ushers in trust and valuing people creates an environment that everyone knows that they matter, faith speaks of victory and a brighter future. Leaders with unwavering faith bring calmness in uncertainty, clear the smog of the present hardships, shine light through the darkness of disappointments; they present to the people a brighter future despite the current circumstances.

Undergirding Churchill's courage was unwavering faith. Faced with an ordeal of the most grievous kind, the Nazi German who wanted to destroy freedom, Churchill promised his newly formed government that they would fight with all the might and strength that God would give them. Most importantly, in the shadow of many months of struggle and suffering, he promised his people victory. When asked what his government's aim was, he is quoted saying, *"It is victory, victory at all costs, victory in spite of all terror, victory, however long and hard the road may be; for without victory there is no survival."* It's this kind of faith that makes a leader courageous.

Whether you are leading your family to a brighter future or leading your team or organization in an ever-fast-changing world with very few predictable events, you can only have unwavering faith if you're standing on a solid ground of integrity, valuing people, and most importantly placing your faith in God. As we can infer from Churchill's words above, God is the source of strength and might when we are faced with challenges.

Colin Powell, retired four-star American Army general stated, *"Leadership is solving problems."* To add to that, I would say that leadership is solving problems for others and with others. I ask you to go and apply the three principles you have learned and soon, you will start to notice that your courage to lead is increasing. I promise you as you become a courageous leader, your success in life will multiply.

6

Productivity: Effort to Impact

"Productivity is never an accident. It is always the result of a commitment to excellence, intelligent planning and focused effort."—Paul J. Meyer

In an interview done for a Netflix documentary, *Inside Bill's Brain: Decode Bill Gates*, the interviewer asked Bill Gates' Executive Administrators, "Is he on time?" referring to Bill Gates.

She replied, *"He is on time to the minute every single meeting without fail."*

Then she added, *"Time is the one commodity that he can't buy more of. It's a limited resource. It's finite. He's got the same 24 hours in a day that the rest of us have."*

As I write this and reflect on Bill's interview, we have spent 353 days so far this year and the one major question that is at the center of my mind is this, **w**hat's the value of the time that we have got in our hands?

Without much debate, we can agree that time is one of the most precious nonrenewable resources we are all given to use, exploit, and utilize with all other resources. With time you can dig out gold. You can refine crude oil into different petroleum products. And most importantly you need time to tap into and expand your second most valuable resource, your mind. Time is the main thing that you must have to be productive. And productivity is the true indicator of the value of time.

To be the richest person on the planet for years, Bill Gates uses the two most valuable resources, time and the mind, to produce the highest value through Microsoft and the Bill & Melinda Gates Foundation and improve the quality of many people's lives. This provides us the definition of productivity, which is the ability to use the resource(s) we have to generate more value in order to positively impact lives.

Further into the interview I referenced above, Bill Gates advised, *"You have to pick a pretty finite number of things to tell your mind to work on. You should decide what you should care about."*

In essence, Gates was unveiling the first step to productivity given that we all have the same amount of time, deliberateness. Anybody can be busy, but not everyone can be productive. Busyness doesn't really need anyone's effort, but being productive calls for one's intentionality. It requires deliberate thinking and actions.

> ***Anybody can be busy, but not everyone can be productive.***

You have to be deliberated on three key areas:

1. Staying Organized.
Looking for misplaced items is an enemy to productivity.

Being productive at any work requires us to use time in the most efficient way. But whenever we take time out of what's important to look for something that is misplaced, we are not being efficient with our time. Staying organized is the antidote for not wasting time looking for misplaced items. As simple as keeping your workstation neat might look, it can improve your productivity significantly.

Staying organized helps productivity in three major ways. *First*, it helps you find things easily and faster. Placing items in designated places, whether tangible items such as tools or intangible items like your files on a computer, will greatly save you a lot of effort when it comes to retrieving them for use. *Second*, it smoothens the workflow. Whenever you take time to look for something that is not immediately available, your thoughts are taken away from the important work to a less important task that could have been avoided if there was some organization. *Third*, it eliminates potential distractions. From experience, I have discovered that any time I step away or leave what I am doing to go in search of something, I find other things that grab my attention away from the important work. We get distracted easily with unimportant tasks when we are not organized. Finding the best way to stay organized, wherever your workspace is, will enable you to make the best of the time you have and also will support the second key to productivity, a disciplined life.

2. Choosing a Disciplined Life.

Choosing a disciplined life means directing your life in accomplishing what you set out to do. It is sticking to a task until you get the results you want. It's impossible to be productive without being disciplined. It is when you have conquered the temptation to quit or you have not allowed yourself to be lulled into inaction by fear of failure, that you have tapped into the second key to productivity, a disciplined life.

Discipline will always outperform intelligence. As the greatest investor of our time, Warren Buffett, once said *"We don't have to be smarter than the rest; we have to be more disciplined than the rest."* With discipline, you can put yourself through a learning process, such as going through school, so as to achieve what you wanted to achieve. Also, it is with discipline that the smartest people can learn the patience to produce results. Being the smartest person doesn't always mean achieving anything. In other words, we can agree with Jim Rohn's statement, *"Discipline is the bridge between goals and accomplishments."* It allows anyone to achieve productivity in their lives.

Discipline is something you are born devoid of. It is something you choose and weave into who we are. I tend to think of it as a muscle that you must develop. Anytime you choose to do what is important and difficult over what is less important and easy, you begin to develop a disciplined life.

When you weave discipline in your life, it aids your productivity in two major ways. *First,* it helps you set your priorities and keep them. S*econd,* it helps you develop persistence, which is crucial for sustained productivity in life. What's even more important about choosing a disciplined life is that it allows you to start using the third key to productivity; focus on a task until it is completed.

3. Focus on a task until it is complete.

A task can never be classified as productive, not unless it is completed. This could be measured in product output or milestones achieved. Remaining focused on a task until it is completed is the third key that you must use to experience productivity.

Focusing on an important task means saying no to all other tasks. It is focusing all your resources on a finite objective until you achieve the best possible results. Apple Inc. founder, Steve Jobs, was known to have said no to hundreds of potential products that the company could have made in order to produce the few superior products that they are known for. He said, *"people think focus means saying yes to the thing you've got to focus on. But that's not what it means at all. It means saying no to the hundred other good ideas that there are."* The way I look at it is, whenever you say yes to one thing, it automatically means you say no to all other things. Therefore, I always remind myself to be very careful with my yeses.

Focusing on a task is important to productivity since it allows us to direct all our efforts to one thing until we get results. Remember this, focusing on a single task with all your effort is like converging the sun's rays on a paper using a magnifying glass until a fire is started.

When you stay organized, choose a disciplined life, and remain focused on a task until it is completed, you will develop a habit of never stopping until your goals are achieved. The habit of sticking to a goal or a task until it's completed is the master key that the super successful people use for productivity.

Energy Maximizing Habits

As the world scrambles for renewable energy sources to meet the growing demand, there seems to be another energy crisis that seems to lack adequate attention, personal energy crisis. We live in an age where the load in our to-do-list is increasingly becoming longer and demanding more from us. The responsibilities both at home and our workplace have led us to live in a state of continuous tiredness. Personal energy crisis is clearly marked with two major things that are impossible to ignore, increased dependency on energy drinks such as Red Bull and the rise of anxiety across all ages of people, showing up as agitation, aggressiveness, and impatience. But like the world energy crisis, the root of this personal energy crisis is poor management of personal energy.

Good management of your personal energy is tied to two things, your awareness, and your habits. One of the important features on any smartphone is often located on the top right corner of the phone's screen. It's the battery icon that tells you the status of your phone's battery: it makes you aware of the energy left before your next charging session. Similar to how we keep an eye on the battery status of our new phones to prevent them from abruptly dying on us, we need to have a means by which we remain aware of our life personal energy before we experience burnout, which is equivalent to a phone dying while in use.

Awareness of your personal energy begins with the knowledge and appreciation of the four quadrants for personal energy abbreviated as the 4QPE, consisting of physical, emotional, mental, and spiritual energies. Unlike the phone that runs on a single battery, we run on a four-chambered battery. Insufficient power in any of the four chambers will only make you run so long before you experience a burnout.

Similar to how we are accustomed to feeling physical fatigue and thereby resting, we ought to equally pay attention to the other three chambers of our batteries. Otherwise stated, we must be aware of the state of our emotional, mental, and spiritual energy as much are very aware of our physical energy.

What's even more valuable is realizing that if we properly manage the emotional, mental, and spiritual chamber, our physical chamber becomes easy to manage. Unfortunately, we pay more attention to our physical state compared to emotional, mental, or spiritual state. We must ask ourselves what habits we must practice or avoid in order to manage the 4QPE.

When it comes to personal energy, habits either drain or recharge our batteries. After having an all-round awareness of your personal energy and realizing that your productivity depends on it, you can develop habits that will help you maximize your personal energy in all four quadrants. These habits include:

1. Resting and Recharging; Protect your resting time.

As simple as this sounds, resting and recharging is becoming increasingly rare and valuable. Rare because what used to be a safe space and time for resting and recharging has been invaded by technology. If you take your phone to bed or have a TV in your bedroom then, technology has infiltrated your resting and recharging space and time. Resting and recharging is becoming more valuable because it's the only means through which we attain mental sharpness and alertness in a world full of distractions.

When it comes to physical and mental resting, I use six hours of uninterrupted sleep between 11:00 pm to 5:00 am. To rest and recharge mentally, in addition to the six hours when I am asleep, I allow reading or watching something that allows me to relax. And what I consider the foundational chamber of my energy, my spiritual energy, I use prayer and fellowship with others of my faith to rest and recharge. This is how I make sure I receive a comprehensive rest and recharge for me to fire on all cylinders.

The question I have for you is this, how do you rest and recharge your four-energy chambers for maximum personal energy? And what is the quality of your rest and recharging time and space? Without proper resting and recharging habits, it will be impossible to exercise the second habit for maximizing your personal energy, exercising inner calmness in every situation.

2. Exercising Inner Calmness in every situation.

The last place to expect calmness is in battlefields where our troops are always under constant pressure of imminent attacks. Yet Former Navy SEAL Commander, Rorke Denver, a man who was trained to be at the heart of the battle said that one of the most valuable advice he ever received in SEAL Training school was on calmness, which was, **calm is contagious.** On the surface, this advice doesn't even remotely connect to the warrior he was being trained to be. But looking closely, a state of calmness keeps at bay its opposite and alternate state, panic. While calmness allows us to focus our energy, panic disperses energy making us ineffective under pressure. This explains why warriors such as men in the Navy SEALs are trained to be calm under stressful environments.

Calmness is an inside condition that comes with lots of exercise. It's maintaining a clear head when there is chaos all around you. You can only exercise inner calmness when you know how to do two things. *First,* being a minimalist when it comes to having control. Understanding that you can control a limited number of things when chaos arises, will help you to give up controlling things that are out of your control and focus on the very few things that you still can control. Often, the few things we can really control lay within us such as our mental state. *Second* is learning to ride the storms of life instead of fighting it. If you learn how to take advantage of the storm, like an eagle, you won't waste any energy fighting the storm, but you will use it to soar higher.

Exercising calmness in all situations will prevent you from being sucked up into the noises of life. It enables you to think and see things clearly thereby allowing you to move with precision. Those who don't remain calm especially in relationships end up misusing their energy engaging in arguments that drain them.

> *If you learn how to take advantage of the storm, like an eagle, you won't waste any energy fighting the storm, but you will use it to soar higher.*

3. Avoid unprofitable arguments.

If there is anything that can quickly and simultaneously drain all your four energy chambers is unprofitable arguments. The writer of some of the most influential letters in history, the Apostle Paul, often warned the men he mentored to be transformative leaders concerning foolish arguments.

In a letter to a young leader named Timothy, the Apostle Paul wrote, *"Avoid foolish and ignorant arguments, knowing that they generate strife,"* 2 Timothy 2:23 (NKJV).

His advice might be a few hundred years old but its truth is undeniable. Despite your cultural or religious background, unprofitable arguments lead to strife and drain all parties' energies. To stay away from unprofitable arguments, we must remember that people have different perspectives depending on their past and present experiences. Sometimes giving people time to gain the insight you have is all the remedy for arguments, especially in a relationship. Giving up the need to always prove that you're right will also save you a lot of energy.

As much as our personal energy is renewable, it's not unlimited. If we are to experience productivity at the highest level, we must manage and protect our four-chambers of personal energy equally since they are dependent on each other. Protect your resting time, intentionally exercise calmness under stressful situations, and never engage in unprofitable arguments. You will maximize your personal energy for productivity.

> ***Giving up the need to always prove that you're right will also save you a lot of energy.***

Time Maximizing Habits

Have you ever wondered why people get so excited about a new year? The answer is obvious. Over the years people have associated a new year with a reset button. A new year triggers a feeling of hope and joy. It is a season where people look forward with great optimism. While this is the case for a new year, it is also true for anytime we get into a new venture, relationship, or relocating to a new city because reset means refocusing and readjusting. However, by pressing the reset button, a sense of urgency kicks in, you begin to consider how much time you need to get results.

How often do you wish you had more time to accomplish your goals? *"I don't have enough time!"* has become a common statement even among young people. It's as though our days no longer have 24 hours. What's still true is that both the productive-successful people and the busy-unproductive have the same amount of time per day to achieve their goals. With that backdrop of truth, you must ask yourself, *what habits will enable you to be effective with our time, especially as you reset and readjust?*

I have found the following three habits to be critical in making sure people maximize their time regardless of their background, success, or goals.

1. Decluttering.

The nature of your environment is a major determining factor on how effective you use your time. A well-organized environment translates to better use of time, while an unorganized environment means the opposite; time is wasted. As I mentioned earlier, effective use of time and productivity are linked by staying organized. Decluttering is the process of keeping our environment free from unwanted stuff. This habit of removing unnecessary things from your environment is the first habit that will allow you to be effective with your time.

There are three environments that directly and daily dictate how our time is consumed. They are, the **mind**, **daily working space**, and our **relationships**. These environments must be decluttered for us to be successful.

First, we declutter our minds by determining the thoughts we allow in our mind. Not every thought that enters your mind should be allowed to settle in. Every thought that comes to you must be judged right. Determine its origins and access its profitability.

Second, we declutter our relationships by being intentional about who we welcome in our lives. The great single-handed influence in your environment is the people in your life. Your relationships determine how you spend your time. When you surround yourself with toxic relationships, you spend your time doing things that are toxic. But when you are surrounded with positive and healthy relationships, you do things that are productive and healthy. So, declutter in the area of relationships by moving away from unhealthy and unproductive relationships.

Third, declutter your workspace. In the digital world we live in, we find ourselves working more digitally than before. This has created a need for us to learn how to declutter that world. Like traditional working space, I have discovered decluttering digitally is very similar to how we clear our physical workspace. Getting rid of unnecessary subscriptions, closing unnecessary web pages, and adopting an easy-to-find filling system is the best way to stay organized.

Decluttering is a powerful habit that enables us to be successful in the few things that are important to us. Its power is well summed up by Joshua Becker, the author of *The More of Less*, in his quote, *"The first step in crafting the life you want is to get rid of everything you don't."* But you can't get rid of what you don't want unless you are okay with saying no!

2. Being Okay With Saying No!

I love serving others. My goal in life is to add value to as many people as I can. So, over the years I found myself being a yes man. But closer observation led me to discover that despite having all the good desire to serve others, if I didn't learn how to say no back then, I would experience burnout. Which is the biggest threat to anyone who serves others. After learning from the stories of successful people, I discovered that saying no was critical to being successful in their purpose.

Saying no in a way that enables you to serve others without being selfish begins with knowing your purpose, commitments, and your boundaries. When you know your purpose, it's easier to say no to things that aren't connected to your values. When you know what you're committed to then saying no to things that distract you from your goals becomes a no-brainer. And when you know where your boundaries are, it's saying no that helps you remain within those boundaries, in an area where you perform at your level best.

But the best benefit to learning how to say no in life is that it allows us to develop the third habit of success, which is living by priority.

3. Living by Priority.

> *"Things which matter most must never be at the mercy of things which matter least."—Johann Wolfgang.*

While decluttering helps you eliminate the unimportant things in life and saying no helps you protect them, living by priority allows you to place the important things front and center and act on them first. It prevents us from falling victim to what the

American prolific Author of *The 7 Habits of Highly Effective People* warned, *"Most of us spend too much time on what is urgent and not enough time on what is important."*

To live by priority calls for you to have three things. First, you must have **a sense of definiteness of purpose**. This allows you to go through life living and standing for something, preventing you from drifting through life. "Definiteness of purpose," as the late Businessman and philanthropist William Clement Stone said, *"is the starting point of all achievement."*

Second, is **a sense of direction**. Often, many people waste a lot of time in a state of stagnation because they don't know which direction they ought to move in. The key to having a sense of direction in life is not knowing the whole journey, but rather knowing and taking the immediate right move to accomplish your purpose. Zig Ziglar well identified the gap between time and direction when he stated, *"Lack of direction, not lack of time, is the problem. We all have twenty-four-hour days."*

Third, to live by priority we need to possess **a sense of urgency**. I will be the first person to admit that when you lack a sense of urgency, you run the risk of experiencing anxiety when deadlines approach. It's a sense of urgency that protects us from the law of diminishing intent, which states, the longer you wait to do something you should do now, the greater the odds that you will never actually do it. Jim Rohn was right when said, *"Without a sense of urgency, desire loses its value."*

While setting out to accomplish your vision and goals, remember that it's by decluttering your life, saying no to the unimportant things that appear as urgent, and living by priority that will allow you to maximize your time on what really matters. You will be productive at work, find more time to spend with your family, and experience growth in your personal life.

Make a Difference with Action

It's not how much money you make that brings fulfillment. It's connecting what you do with your purpose that brings great fulfillment in life. It's doing (performing) a seemingly insignificant act of difference in an area or field that you believe will make the greatest difference to humanity at large. Taking action in what you believe in is what leads to a life that brings you joy.

Fulfillment doesn't happen at the end of life, it happens in the journey of life. According to Bronnie Ware, a former palliative care giver and author of bestselling book, *5 Regrets of the Dying*, dreams not acted upon is the biggest regret people faced on their deathbed. Taking action is what produces great value in our lives. '

Amazon Founder, Jeff Bezos, would still be under someone else's payroll, but he mustered the courage to quit his job to pursue what he believed to be the greatest opportunity in front of him back in 1994. Interestingly, in an interview much earlier before Bronnie Ware's list was published, Jeff Bezos had an insight on how action leads to fulfillment and eliminates regrets. He shared about a mindset he referred to as the *regret minimization framework* that helped him take action to start what has become one of the most successful businesses in our century. Basically, the mindset helped him take action in the present to avoid regret in the future.

The greatest enemy to action is fear. Fear prevents most people from living a life that's truly fulfilling. It can tie people down in jobs they hate and force them to remain in the shallow end of performance, mediocre work. Despite the position or kind of job one has, fear has the ability to breed inaction even in the best of ideas. While fear will always be there, courage is what silences its call for inaction. Courage calls you into action in the midst of judgment and criticism from others, and even when failure is possible.

> *While fear will always be there, courage is what silences its call for inaction.*

I am convinced that to take action that produces great work, courage is required. My goal is to show you how to build courage to take action(s) that will propel you to producing work that will bring you fulfillment. The question of *how do you show up and perform at your best without fear of failing* has helped me discover three mindsets on developing courage to make a difference with action. Let's examine each mindset:

1. Embrace Excellence.

I grew up hearing the words excellence, but my poor understanding of excellence made me think it was only for a select few. I thought it was only for the top students in my class or for the fellow employee who was the most experienced at my workplace. I believed that excellence meant I had to be perfect. But all that changed when I realized that excellence was not something that people are born with but a habit that people developed, and I could develop it as well. Most importantly, I learned that excellence didn't require perfection, but for me to be in a state of continuous improvement. This realization made me embrace excellence by putting in me a desire to be excellent. I immediately started working on it.

Not long after this, I noticed a shift in how I approach any task or work I was engaged in. I realized that the fear of failing was shrinking and my desire to learn was increasing. I stopped paying attention to the critics and naysayers. Rather, I cared more about improving and getting better as a person. This was followed by increased courage to take on actions that were at times more challenging, demanding and at other times beyond my abilities. This is when I discovered that the step of building courage for action was embracing excellence; being in a continuous state of improvement.

You embrace excellence when you make it a habit. That is, when you become intentional on doing better than your last attempt. You become your greatest competitor. When this happens, you will soon tap into the unlimited power of excellence to boost your courage to make a difference by your action. Excellence will not only boost your courage, it will direct you to a craftsman mindset, as discussed in Cal Newport's book, *So Good They Can't Ignore You*.

A craftsman mindset will allow what embracing excellence produces to be channeled into deliberate practice. It allows you to focus on what's important and maximize your practice to become your best. While embracing excellence ignites courage, possessing a make-a-difference mindset amplifies courage.

2. Possess a Make-a-Difference Mindset.

The 2004 Nobel Peace Prize winner, Wangari Maathai Ph.D., a Kenyan-born environmentalist, referred to herself as a hummingbird. She was fond of giving the hummingbird story during her interviews. The story is about a huge fire that had engulfed a forest. All the wild animals ran out of the forest and stood at a distance. All animals were hopelessly looking at the fire consuming the forest, feeling overwhelmed and powerless except a little hummingbird.

"I'm going to do something about the fire!" It shouted.

Without hesitation, it flew to the nearest stream, took a drop of water and put it on the fire. It went up and down, as fast as it could. But as it was flying back and forth, all the other animals, even the much bigger animals like the elephant that could have carried much more water with their long trunks, were standing there helpless.

They would say to the hummingbird, *"What do you think you can do? You are too little. This fire is too big. Your wings are too little, and your beak is so small that you can only bring a small drop of water at a time."*

But as they continued to discourage it, it turned to them and without wasting any time said, *"I am doing the best I can."*

Despite its tiny size in comparison to the fire, the hummingbird exemplifies what it means to possess a *make-a-difference mindset*. It believed that what it had or what it could do could make a difference. It did not wait for the rest of the animals to take action. Like the bird, don't wait to have the best plan or tools to believe you can make a difference; start with what you have.

Possessing a make-a-difference mindset will shift your focus from fear to what you can do. It will amplify the courage and help you to take action and get started like the hummingbird.

3. Focus on getting started.

The final step to developing courage to make a difference with action is to get started. You can never finish a journey of a thousand steps if you don't take the first step. This is where I would like to remind you that courage is not a feeling, but it's an action. We don't feel courageous, rather, we act courageous.

Getting started is what gives fear the Mike Tyson TKO. It's the straw that breaks the camel's back of fear and stagnancy. It ignites the momentum of subsequent actions that fear cannot stop. Getting started is like pushing the first piece of a domino.

I focus on getting started in every process using this question, *What's the right and easiest thing I can do now to achieve my bigger goal?* Try using this question next time you feel overwhelmed by a big goal.

Now that you have learned the steps required to develop courage for action and be productive, I would like you to identify an area of your life where you can make a difference by taking action and acting immediately. Finally, as you go into the next chapter, I would like to share with you a statement a friend once said to me:

> ***No one can progress in life without courage to act.***

It is this statement that always inspired me to develop courage for action in my life. When people get jammed by fear of failure and become less productive, you courage to act will be what makes all the difference in your journey.

7

Faith: See Into The Unseen

"Faith gives you an inner strength and a sense of balance and perspective in life."—Gregory Peck

Walking by faith is the single most powerful quality that will enable you to do things you thought were impossible and take you to places you hadn't imagined. It will open the doors of abundance and unlock your potential. But walking by faith requires vision. It's impossible to take a step of faith without vision. The writer of the book of Hebrews in the bible offered the best definition of faith. *"Faith is the substance of things hoped for, the evidence of things not seen"* Hebrews 11:1 (KJV). The second half of this definition, evidence of things not seen, is only possible by vision. Therefore, vision is the prerequisite for walking by faith.

Vision is the ability to see beyond what's on the surface or the current conditions. It's seeing beyond what your natural sight enables us to see. Vision provides us with the reasons to take action in our present moment to create a new reality. It also ignites in us the courage to take the steps of faith.

Walking by faith is taking the steps towards what you have visualized. It's taking actions that will lead to achieving what you hope for. It's making decisions that align your current actions to your future desired outcome. Often, whenever we hear people talking about walking by faith, we tend to think it's always referring to the big moves in life, but what I have discovered is that walking by faith is not measured by the size of steps taken but rather by number of steps taken. Whether it's taking a small or big step, or making a small or big decision, What counts is that we are moving towards what we envision. There are three keys that must be in place if we are going to walk by faith to fulfill our vision.

1. Hope of the invisible.

The first key to walking by faith is having hope. The first section of the definition of faith above, faith is the substance of things hoped, shows that hope is the connector of visible and invisible things. Hope is the bloodline of walking by faith. While walking by faith is taking actions (visible), hope is the roadmap that directs us from within towards our desires (invisible). We move to places of hope. We act because there is hope our actions can bring change. Where there is no hope there is inaction and destitution looms.

The opposite of walking by faith is walking by fear. Fear clouds our thinking and makes us walk in the dark. But when we choose hope, fear dissipates. Hope shines light in the darkness and guides our steps.

Hope not only guides us, it also brings forth belief. It ignites in us passion for something in the present moment that looks impossible. With hope in place you unlock the second key to walking by faith, which is believing you can do the impossible.

2. Believe you can do the impossible.

While hope is the bedrock to walking by faith and guides our steps, belief is the energy through which we make the steps; It powers the steps we take to achieve greatness and it is the second key to walking by faith.

Believing you can do the impossible empowers you to walk by faith in three ways. *First, it activates your willpower.* Your willingness to do anything is dependent on whether you believe in possibilities. You are automatically unwilling to do what you don't believe to be possible. When your belief activates your willpower, you become confident in starting and following through on your goals. *Second,* believing you can do the impossible will *activate your imagination.* Imagination is dull where there is no belief. Believing in making the impossible possible activates your mental faculties to start generating new ideas. *Third,* believing in doing the impossible *activates your creativity.* Imagination and creativity increase our capacity to start seeing new possibilities when you are faced with what might seem to be impossible to others. When these three, willpower, imagination, and creativity are activated, you will realize something significant. You need others in the journey of conquering mountains, doing the impossible things of life. You also need fellowship with people of faith, which is the third key to walking by faith.

3. Fellowship with people of faith.

Walking by faith is a behavior that is adoptable. Not one person is born knowing how to walk by faith. In whatever situation that you have ever walked by faith, you learned how to from someone else. You learned how to believe in the impossible when you watched your parents or close friends choose to remain hopeful in hopeless situations; when they decided to take actions that at the moment seemed to yield no results, and what they believed in themselves to do things that seemed like a mountain. Keeping fellowship with people of faith is setting yourself up to pick up the habits that encourage walking by faith. Fellowship is not limited to religious settings. Fellowship is any company of people we keep of whom our energies resonate in the same frequency.

While we can classify hope and believe as potential energy for walking by faith, fellowship is what turns that potential energy into kinetic energy. People of faith, through fellowship, will turn your potential energy into kinetic energy or in other words make you an action-oriented person in three ways.

First, they feed your faith. The people around us can only feed us with two powerful emotions, fear or faith. While people who feed you with fear will always tell you what's impossible, people of faith will feed your faith through encouragement by showing you the possibilities.

Second, they create a positive atmosphere around you. People of faith always have an elevated perspective in life. They view life in a positive way because they understand that there is already too much negativity in the world. They speak of possibilities and hope in light of hopeless situations. They think of what is true, noble, right, pure, lovely, admirable and things that are of excellence or praiseworthy report. When you are around such people, you will know because you will leave encouraged because of the positive atmosphere they create.

Third and most important, they direct you to resources. The most transformative benefit of having fellowship with people of faith is that they are always supportive. While people of fear are always fixated on the impossible, people of faith see possibilities for themselves and others around them. This always leads them to naturally find resources to help them accomplish their vision. When we are in the company of people of faith, they are quick to point us to the direction of resources.

Whenever our faith is fed, a positive atmosphere is created. We are directed to resources. We are empowered to take the step of faith in response to the hope of the invisible we see through vision. And we begin to act on our belief of doing the impossible. We begin to walk by faith.

Traveling Light

After traveling quite often, I have learned how to travel light. I carefully choose everything I take with me. I go to the extent of carefully considering what to wear because of going through the TSA security. I have learned that the less I carry with me, the more I get to enjoy the journey. While we put much thought on making our airport experience easier, maybe by wearing comfortable shoes or by ensuring that our luggage is not over the required airline weight, I have observed that we often don't take as much consideration to the quality of the bigger journey we all are in, the journey of life. Particularly, we don't pay attention to what we carry in our journey until it becomes too heavy for us to bear. While we don't like to get stopped by the TSA agent for something suspicious in our bags, we completely hate having to pay extra for overweight bags. Similarly, we shouldn't wait until the price tag for what we carry through in life is too much for us to bear. To avoid this happening and assure you enjoy your life, you must, at one point or another, answer the question, *what's necessary for me to carry on the journey of life?*

In the wake of July 15th, 1994, what had been viewed by the global community as an internal conflict had resulted in the mass execution of about one million people and an estimated five hundred thousand rapes. The members of the Tutsi tribe were nearly wiped out from the face of the earth by their fellow countrymen of the Hutu tribe. The Rwandan genocide, its scale and brutality, caused shock worldwide. Families that had lived alongside each other for years and their children played together, had now taken up arms against each other. The whole world wondered how all the hurts would ever be reconciled.

But today, over 25 years after the devastating war that left a country deeply scarred and the world utterly shocked, Rwanda is defining forgiveness. Thousands of perpetrators are living alongside their victims. The deep wounds that seemed impossible to overcome, are now being healed across the country one victim at a time. Perpetrators are seeking forgiveness to their victims, while victims are seeking healing. The result is a healing nation.

Over the years, the people of Rwanda, had to answer the question, what was necessary for them to carry moving forward, hurting or healing? They chose healing. Healing required them to choose one of the oldest ways for lightening the burden of life; Forgiveness. In this world, you will fail, you will find faults in others, and you will be hurt by others. Failure, faults, and hurts are the greatest source of extra weight we might pick on this journey of life. But like the Rwandan people, if we live a life of forgiveness, we will have taken the first step of traveling light.

So, before we can dive into how forgiveness lightens our journey, let's examine what are the core factors of forgiveness that allows it to lighten our lives as it's doing for the people of Rwanda.

1. A Heart of Love.

"There is no love without forgiveness, and there is no forgiveness without love," Bryant McGill, author of the *Voice of Reason*. It is impossible to separate forgiveness from love. Mother Teresa, 1979 Nobel Peace Prize, who was known for her life of service is quoted saying, *"If we really want to love, we must learn how to forgive."* If you have ever forgiven anyone, whether you consider them a friend or not, your forgiveness originated from love. Whether you were conscious of the love or not. A heart devoid of love is full of hate, and where there is hate there is no forgiveness. Therefore, at the core of true and pure forgiveness is a heart of love.

A heart of love, that is a heart that is filled with love, even when faced with failure, faults, or hurts of others, is able to withstand all evil. One of my favorite prolific writers, Apostle Paul, described love by giving its attribute that showed what love was and what it wasn't. In describing what it is, he wrote, *"love is patient and it is kind."* In referencing what it isn't he wrote, *"Love does not envy, isn't boastful, or proud. It does not dishonor others, it is not self-seeking, it is not easily angered, it keeps no record of wrongs....always hopes, always perseveres and love never fails."* These qualities of love explain why a heart that's full love is at the core of forgiveness. While love opens the doors for forgiveness, grace powers us to take the actions of forgiveness.

2. The Power of Grace.

Forgiveness is about deliberate and decisive actions that bring healing to the soul. The gap between deciding to forgive and letting go of the pain and bitterness is only closed by the power of grace. Grace is unmerited or underserved kindness. When we get hurt by people, the first virtue that gets affected is kindness. But grace moves us to forgive despite the fact that those hurt us don't deserve it.

The work of Photographer Pieter Hugo of South Africa was featured on New York Times Magazine (online) in which he documented stories of reconciliation in Rwanda 20 years after the genocide. The trend that emerged in every story was how grace from the survivors was extended to the perpetrators of the war. There was nothing that could be done to bring healing to the people apart from forgiveness powered by grace. No prison time was able to cleanse the sins of the offenders.

Karorero, a survivor of the genocide is quoted saying, *"Sometimes justice does not give someone a satisfactory answer. But when it comes to forgiveness willingly granted, one is satisfied once and for all."* This is what grace does. It allows us to extend forgiveness to those who might never be able to pay us back. Karorero added, *"When someone is full of anger, he can lose his mind. But when I granted them forgiveness, I felt my mind at rest."*

It is only when we allow the power of grace to move us, that we are able to forgive. Lasting forgiveness that eliminates any traces of bitterness is only possible by grace. And when we yield to the power of grace, we are moved from a state of bitterness to a place where we desire reconciliation.

3. A Desire for Reconciliation.

Forgiveness always seeks a positive outcome. At the core of

forgiveness is a desire for reconciliation. Reconciliation does not mean forgetting what has happened in the past, but it is acknowledging the failures we have experienced, the faults of others, and the hurts we have experienced in our past, then moving into the future in the most positive way possible.

While it is true that we may not be able to restore every broken relationship to its former state, we can build stronger and more beautiful relationships when we fully allow the process of forgiveness to take its course. It's us who hold back and stand in the way of forgiveness. There is no forgiveness if there is something that's holding us back.

Circling back to where we began, when we forgive, we do it because of the heart of love; it forms a loop that births a deep human desire for reconciliation. So, when you listen deeply to the heart of forgiveness, there is a desire for reconciliation.

Forgiveness is a result of love, grace, and a desire to reconcile. In Rwanda, it's not only healing the two tribes, it's also allowing Rwandans, whether Tutsi or Hutu, to have a better view of each other and look into the future of their country with hope. As a result, Rwanda has overcome its dark past and has emerged as one of the most successful economies in Africa.

Forgiveness is the first key to traveling light.

Power of Forgiveness

> *"I felt something very heavy lifted off my chest,"* my mom deeply sighed with her eyes smiling at me.

Growing up, like many families, we had a rough patch that almost tore our family apart. At the center of the pain of the family disputes was a family-friend we greatly honored. The lies, insults, and confusion they had brought to our family were directed at my mother. It was so bad that most of our extended family distanced themselves from us.

I vividly remember one morning when things turned from bad to worse, my parent's argument spilled out of the safety net they had created for us not to be exposed to what was going on. Being a little older than my younger brother, I was terrified that our family would fall victim of divorce.

But at that tipping-point, while any rational person would have thought it was the end of our family, my mum did the unexpected. Instead of blaming anyone for the predicament we were in, she became very intentional about praying, protecting us, and seeking to forgive anyone that was involved in bringing us pain, including the family friend who was the epicenter of it all.

In hindsight, I learned two important lessons on forgiveness from this memory. *First,* I learned that forgiveness is possible despite how bad the hurt and failure was. *Second,* forgiveness can heal the deepest wounds of being wronged, especially by those who you least expected to hurt you. But before I share with you how forgiveness lightens your life, especially in light of your past hurts, failures, and disappointments, let's look at five misconceptions about forgiveness that keep most people from benefiting from forgiveness.

Misconceptions of Forgiveness

- **Forgiveness requires an apology.** *"I will not forgive them until they come to me and apologize."* This kind of self-talk has kept many captive to their negative experiences. Forgiveness doesn't not require an apology. Often, when people wrong you, the last thing they want to do is face you. This means they will unlikely come to you and say sorry. And if they do come, their forgiveness might not be adequate for what they did. So anytime you wait for an apology, it might take forever to come, and if it ever comes, it might not be what you expected. Therefore, never wait for an apology, forgive first.
- **When you forgive, you benefit your offender.** Forgiveness is first and foremost important for you. The ultimate benefit for forgiveness is healing and you are the first recipient of this benefit. Your offender is a secondhand beneficiary of what forgiveness does for you.
- **You must recover from a hurt before you forgive.** While this looks like the order of events when it comes to forgiveness, it's not exactly accurate. Forgiveness is the first step to healing and recovering from any past hurts. Avoiding someone or ignoring a pain someone caused you would be like addressing the symptoms of a disease, but forgiving is the surgery that leads to healing, as it addresses the root cause of the pain.
- **If you forgive, the offense will be repeated.** This misconception is born out of fear of being hurt again. But whenever

forgiveness happens, and especially if the offender is aware of it, its power transforms their attitude towards a very positive one.

- **Forgiveness means you shouldn't or can't address the hurt with your offender.** One way to look at forgiveness is looking at it as a door, a door that brings healing and reconciliation. It's only when you go through the door of forgiveness that you are able to address the issue that caused you hurt in a wholesome way. Without forgiveness, bitterness and resentment will prevent you from facing the issues clearly.

It's only when we don't fall for the above misconceptions about forgiveness, that we are able to fully benefit from the power of forgiveness and its ability to lighten our journey through life. Forgiveness enables us to travel light in life in the following three ways:

1. Refresh your perspective on failure and mistakes.

The heaviest load in life you can bear is unreconciled failures and mistakes. *While failure and mistakes are inevitable, learning from them is not a guarantee.* Learning from your failures and mistakes is the way to reconcile them, which requires a different perspective than what leads to them. Forgiveness is what refreshes your perspective on failure and mistakes, thereby allowing you to learn from them. Whether it is a failure you experienced or a wrong done to you by somebody else, forgiving yourself or the other person, enables you to acknowledge what has happened and hit the refresh button on your outlook.

The moment your perspective is refreshed, and you begin looking at your failures and mistakes from a better vantage, you begin to experience the next power of forgiveness, which is the release from past negative experiences.

2. Release your mind from negative experiences.

Going back to my family's story, my mother (mum) would have allowed the negative experience to hold her back, but she chose forgiveness. My mum tells me how when she decided to completely and unconditionally forgive the family friend who was at the center of all the controversies, she decided to approach her and tell her that she had forgiven her. That decision alone set her free from the negative past experiences. She stopped feeling bad or hurt whenever she would see her. All the negative emotions were wiped-out by the simple act of forgiveness. Witnessing firsthand the healing that took place and the peace of mind that followed, taught me that it is very important to use forgiveness to release my mind for any past negative experiences. And it's only when our minds are free from past negative experiences that we are able to have the energy of being in charge of the future.

3. Revamp your energy to take control of the future.

The late radio host Bernard Meltzer of the call-in show, *"What's Your Problem?"* once said, *"When you forgive, you in no way change the past–but you sure do change the future."* Often, the pain caused by others, especially those closest to you, might seem to be too much to leave behind. But when you forgive, there is a magical, almost mystical thing that happens in your heart that gives you energy to turn from the past and face the future. Through forgiveness, you are empowered to have control of the future. Without forgiveness, you become powerless to conquer the past. When it came to my mum, twenty years after the family conflict, she became the cornerstone of the strength of the family because she chose forgiveness.

I shared this intimate story about my family to show you one thing, forgiveness is a powerful force that can heal. Joyce Meyer, an American Christian author, speaker and president of Joyce Meyer Ministries said, *"Forgiveness is not a feeling – it's a decision we make because we want to do what's right before God."* I saw my mum make the tough decision to forgive, and I believe that you have the power to forgive anyone in your life who has caused you pain. Joyce Meyer added, *"It's a quality decision that won't be easy and it may take time to get through the process, depending on the severity of the offense."* To add to the wisdom of Joyce, I would say, as you go through the process, make sure you don't get hindered by the misconceptions we covered above. Remember that with God's help you can forgive anyone.

Unlocking More Blessings

No bad day ever lacks something good to appreciate. There is no season that doesn't have its beauty. Despite the cold weather of winter, there is beauty in snow, and with the heat of summer, comes the attractive flowers and beautifully kept lawns. The year 2020-2021 could easily be remembered in history from a negative view. However, I am convinced that despite the pandemic that disrupted how we lived, and the social injustices we witnessed across the world, there is still plenty to be thankful for. I know that years later, we will mine many valuable lessons that contributed to a better future.

For example, the expedited vaccine development and deployment, meant that scientists broke new grounds in clinical research and development. In addition, when we had to change our social interactions by social distancing and masking up, we learned to endure a little discomfort to make sure we are all safe. Regardless of how your past experiences have been or your current condition is not as you expected, if you look closely, you can always find something valuable to carry forward. But to do this, you have to walk the path of gratitude.

The Path of Gratitude

The path of gratitude has two critical markers; first, faith and hope, and second, a life that focuses on what went right instead of what did not work. The first sign that you are on the path of gratitude is the continued expression of faith and hope for a blessed life. People who have decided to possess a grateful heart and intentionally express gratitude at every turn of their life are optimistic and expect good things in their lives. As a result of having faith and hope, people on the gratitude path focus on what is working and are not stopped with what doesn't.

Our wiring sometimes works against us when we so easily focus on the negative things around us; we look at the misfortunes of life and ignore the good things that happen to us daily. But we don't have to be at the mercy of our wiring, we can reshape how we think about what goes on in our life. The best path to transform your mind is by walking on the path of gratitude. The path of gratitude enables you to focus on your blessings. And because we focus on what went right, the path of gratitude protects us from the time-consuming and energy-wasting exercise of complaining. Complaining and gratitude cannot coexist; It's impossible to complain and be thankful at the same time. As you have faith and hope, focus on what's going well, and don't complain as a result of walking on the path of gratitude, the following life-transforming things will happen that will unlock more blessings to flow in your life.

> ***The best path to transform your mind is by walking on the path of gratitude.***

1. Elevate your outlook.

Several times I have heard people ask, *"how do immigrants come to the U.S from impoverished countries, and after a few years in America, they become financially successful?"* As a person who also immigrated from a third world country, I have had to ponder on this question numerous times. The one thing I believe is the main force behind all the success for immigrants, whether the founding immigrants of the United States or the contemporary ones, is gratitude.

As an immigrant myself, I can confidently say that when people move to the United States, the most successful country in the world, they are filled with a sense of gratitude. They know in this country there are plenty of opportunities that can make their dreams come true. Generally, people who come to the US appreciate the many amenities they enjoy which were not in their countries of origin. Because of their attitude of gratitude, their life's outlook is elevated. I believe this is why America, the nation of immigrants, is a superpower. But the power of gratitude to elevate our outlook does not stop with immigrants. Anyone born anywhere, including the natives, can elevate their outlook by expressing gratitude.

Gratitude will elevate your viewpoint by enabling you to pay attention to what is working instead of what is not. It will allow you to count your blessings regardless how small they appear. When you choose to be grateful over a few things, you discover there are many things for which you can be thankful. Gratitude is an expression of the heart that influences the mind to shift from scarcity to abundance.

2. Sensitize you to abundance.

If there is one person who would have good reasons to focus on the scarcity of their upbringing, it would be a young black woman who was born and brought up in Mississippi in the 1950s, Oprah Winfrey. In spite of the poverty and racism of her time, she rose up to be the most successful black woman in the world. Oprah Winfrey's emphasis on gratitude over the years could explain the larger-than-life success, fame, and fortune she enjoys today. She has often advised in her shows, *"Be thankful for what you have; you'll end up having more. If you concentrate on what you don't have, you will never, ever have enough."*

Your story is not that of Oprah, but what is true is that you live in abundance. The question is, are you aware of it? Being grateful for the few blessings you have is the key to sensitizing yourself to the abundance that God has released for you to enjoy. When God created the universe, He made sure there were enough resources for you to enjoy significant success. Being grateful also attracts more blessings in your life.

While abundance is realized when we live in gratitude, scarcity is created when we fail to be thankful for what we have. Scarcity of resources is nothing more than failure to appreciate the raw materials you have in your hands such as life. It's a mindset of focusing on what you don't readily have and ignoring what's at hand.

The more you operate from a scarcity mindset, the more diseases you create in your life. Diseases that range from poor habits to physical illnesses. But only gratitude can bring healing.

> *While abundance is realized when we live in gratitude, scarcity is created when we fail to be thankful for what we have.*

3. Gratitude brings healing.

Losing something valuable or failing at something important in life is inevitable. It's possible to suffer heartache and headaches the moment loss or failure happens. However, it's not necessary to continue to propagate more heart and mind illness by focusing on what went wrong. You can recover from any pain caused by failures or losses when you seek and find something to be grateful for regardless of how bad things look like. This way, gratitude brings healing to you.

Zig Ziglar said it best, *"Gratitude is the healthiest of all human emotions. The more you express gratitude for what you have, the more likely you will have even more to express gratitude for."* To experience good health, physically, emotionally, or spiritually, you must practice gratitude in your life.

In summary, gratitude is the way to unlock more blessings in our life. It elevates our outlook which prevents us from being consumed by the storms of life and enables us to see great opportunities ahead of where we are today. It makes you aware of the many blessings you have upon which you experience more blessings. And it restores your overall health by enabling you to quickly recover from setbacks.

> *Gratitude is an expression of the heart that influences the mind to shift from scarcity to abundance.*

About the Author

Dr. Samson Gichuki is a Husband, Certified Coach and Speaker. He holds a Ph.D. degree in Biotechnology. Sam's passion is to add value to people through mentorship, coaching, and speaking. His mission is to equip people with the necessary tools for personal growth and leadership development. He serves as the Youth Patron and Bible Study Teacher at his local church. Currently, he resides in the Greater Baltimore area and enjoys reading, traveling, and watching wildlife documentaries.

You can connect with me on:
🌐 https://www.samsongichuki.com

Also by Dr. Samson Gichuki

Victorious Living: A 90-Day Devotional To Spiritual Growth
This devotional is designed to help you uplift your perspective by providing God's view from His word on carefully selected topics. The topics are selected in a way that you will embark on a 90-day journey to spiritual growth. There are questions after each day's topic to help you reflect further.

By the end of the 90-day journey, you will gain biblical and practical skills to serve others. The main goal of this devotional is to help you grow and learn to grow others through serving. Through this book, I pray that the power of God will enable you to lead a victorious life through spending time in the Word, with fellow believers, and serving others.

www.ingramcontent.com/pod-product-compliance
Lightning Source LLC
LaVergne TN
LVHW021829060526
838201LV00058B/3569